I AM THE

MESSENGER

Lynne Cutler

I AM THE MESSENGER
© Lynne Cutler 2017

National Library of Australia Cataloguing-in-Publication entry (pbk)

Author: Cutler, Lynne, author.
Title: I Am The Messenger/ Lynne Cutler
ISBN: 9781925680102 (paperback)
            978-1-925680-11-9 (ebook)
Subjects: Cutler, Lynne.
            Women mediums--Biography
            Spiritual healing--Biography.
            Meditation.

Published by Lynne Cutler and Ocean Reeve Publishing
www.lynnecutlerauthor.com
www.oceanreeve.com

Ocean
REEVE
PUBLISHING

I dedicate this book to my parents who are now in the spirit world and to my two children Ayden and Soffie.

Contents

Acknowledgments

I would like to give thanks and love to the following people:

Anya grabbed my hand during a coffee catch up in 2003, with the intention of reading my palm, whereupon she announced, "You never told me you were writing a book." My decision was made one month earlier and I hadn't mentioned it to anyone.

Bev Kurkowski who was my first editor and yes, there was a lot to change.

During my confabulations with family, I was made aware of certain events and other information.

Debra Jarvis (Yuille) my long term close friend contributed to constructive criticism in the next editing procedure.

Susan Jane introduced me to new ideas in her writing group and has become an esteemed friend. One of her suggestions was to divide the book into two or three. I decided to separate this book into two, although I'm sure there will be a third to follow. She also contributed with photographs throughout the book.

Ocean Reeve for mentoring and encouraging in the publishing process.

Melly Stewart for the photography session in the Japanese gardens at Mt. Cootha with the result being the photograph on the front cover.

John Cutler for the logo on the back cover.

Vicki Oakhill for kinesiology, massage and Bowen technique during my personal development over the many years we have been in contact.

Debbie Leigh for her encouragement in life and health consultations during the 29 years we have known each other.

To all those people who have helped me through the tough times and the good times. These are just a few:- Alleyne, Stephanie, Donna, Dee, Lindal, Lorraine, Jan, Jenny, Pauline, Kate, Jacki, Karen, Layle, Michelle and Vanessa. All the girls and guys at the gym for our coffee catch up after a sweaty workout. I needed the gym workout to release any stress and the social coffee catch up. Also the early Monday walks with a friendly group at Mt. Cootha, followed by breakfast. A great start to the week.

Love and peace to all the people I have touched throughout my life.

My name Lynne means cascade, waterfall.

The rivers, lakes, cascades and waterfalls are so mesmeric to the mind, body and soul, creating calmness and tranquillity to everyone who gazes upon them.

On the other hand, imagine how the water feels and that's how my emotions were as I experienced each life encounter. I felt like I was travelling the river of life where the waterfalls were a big impact in my life.

Foreword

An amazing woman, an incredible gift!

Lynne Cutler is the oldest of six children and it wasn't until after the passing of her mother she acknowledged and really embraced her intuitive/psychic ability to communicate with spirit, allowing space in her life to tune in and share the insights she receives with others. She is a mother of two, daughter, sister, friend and lover who bridges two worlds, the conventional materialistic and the spiritual, mystic world beyond this physical form of life.

Inside this book, you will discover how Lynne opened up to owning her gift, the journey she's travelled because of it and the messages she receives for herself, friends and clients. Lynne is a conduit, a medium that brings messages to our visual physical world from the unseen spiritual realm.

When Lynne learnt to allow herself to be vulnerable, she opened herself up to listening to the messages she received. The messages provided guidance to assist her in living her authentic life every day and to put pen to paper, writing her story to share with you. Listening to her guides, the events in her life became synchronistic, supporting her in material ways to get on with her life's purpose.

As you read Lynne's story which has naïve honesty, you will find yourself relating to her journey and it will inspire you to live your own unique life, following your own special path to fulfilling your potential in this life time. Real, raw and authentic, Lynne is one of life's special people and through this book you will get to know her and in the process look deeply into your own being.

I am so thrilled that this book is finally published. I eagerly anticipate seeing Lynne embark on the next phase of her life, empowering and inspiring many other earth angels to tap into their gifts and live the life they were born to embrace.

Blessings to Lynne and to all those who read this book and are touched by her vision.

Debra Jarvis

We are in relationships for

A Reason

A Season

Or

A Lifetime

My First Spiritual Experience

In September 1985, I thought my river of life was flowing along smoothly as I enjoyed the study involved in becoming a Beauty Therapist. Little did I know that my river of life was due to experience the upheaval and wonderment of a life changing waterfall!

On Tuesday evenings, a doctor gave lectures on Anatomy and Physiology. After the fourth class, my nerve endings were agitated about passing the exam. My thoughts were that the lecturer wasn't giving his students enough information to pass. At that stage I was not aware that a beauty therapist did not need to know as much information as a nurse or doctor. Studying again after 15 years was very daunting, although it really makes a difference if one is totally captivated on the subject matter.

One evening, after finishing my lecture and still feeling on edge, I walked towards my car, down a narrow street with plenty of street lighting and not a soul around. Walking closer to my car, I felt the presence of my mother who had died nearly 10 years previous.

She said, "Don't worry about your exam, as you will pass with high marks."

Immediately my body trembled as my fight/flight response kicked in. I was scared and quickened my pace to the car, just a short distance ahead. The keys were in my hand, so it was relatively easy, (although I was trembling slightly) to put the car key into the key hole and open the door. I slid into the driver's seat as the door slammed, sitting there trembling and breathing with a wheeze, which was representative of having a slight asthma attack. Once composed, my realization was that the presence of my mother wasn't there. I wound down the window and my mother's presence was waiting near my car door. She didn't say anything and neither did I. Her presence stayed for what seemed like minutes although in fact it may have been seconds. My thoughts were that she was waiting for me to accept this situation and once I did, her presence disappeared. The vision of her was not human but was her energy. The energy or presence was instantaneously recognisable although how I knew, was beyond belief.

I sat in the car for at least 15 minutes trying to decipher what had just happened. I felt I was over the waterfall edge and freefalling into the river or abyss.

My mind was racing…Was the stress of my study sending me a little crazy, causing me to have delusions?

Had I really felt the presence of my mother? Had she really spoken to me? How could she? She had been dead for ten years. Had I taken on too much at my ripe old age of 35? I had heard that one becomes more psychic after giving birth to children.

She told me not to worry about my exam. It was definitely her presence and it was very strong. I knew it was her instantly although it was scary. I'm a sceptic. It felt like her and it was her voice, although how could a dead person talk to me? I didn't know! Nevertheless she did, I think…yes it was her – it was definitely her. Wow! What an experience. I pondered on this for a while and then decided to drive home or my husband would wonder about my whereabouts.

Driving home in a bewildered state with no idea how to explain my experience or delay, I decided not to say a word. It wasn't until a few weeks later with the memory still fresh in my mind that I blurted out my experience to my husband. He looked up from the paper he was reading with blankness in his hazel eyes. I don't believe he understood what I was talking about. Gee…did I?

Weeks later, having finished my lectures, it was time for the exam. My anxious thoughts were that I did not know enough to pass this exam. Nevertheless, I passed well with 86%. My mother appeared to allay my stressful thoughts, yet I doubted her words.

This was my first initiation to the spirit world. I was sceptical about the idea of life after death; however now evidence was presented to me. My mother had materialised and spoken to me.

The initial shock of my mother's energy presenting itself was like hitting the base of the waterfall, no longer freefalling and felt nurtured by knowing that there was more to life. This message from my spirit mother turned my river of life into another direction unbeknown to me. The feeling was like going through the rapids.

I didn't realize then, that this was the start of something huge in my life: discoveries about me, who I am and why I am on this planet. The stories I am about to unravel, are absolutely sincere and have surprised me, so much so that my private evolution has steered me to become a spiritual healer. Step by step I have unravelled amazing occurrences which have a significant impact on healing me in this lifetime. This in turn has moved my way of interpreting the challenges of life and our existence. My life passion is to tell the world that this is not our only existence. We come down to earth with the express intention to learn lessons that are not reachable in the spirit world.

Heaven, the spirit world or Universe is full of LOVE and we leave that to experience other emotions on earth.

Travels across the Sea

Let's travel back to before my mother died, to where this story really started. I left the comfort of my family home at age 21 with my sister Sue to travel overseas in a huge Italian ship. This was an exciting adventure for the two of us, travelling by ship over the deep blue seas of relative calm. It brought the travellers on a trip to Fiji, the Panama Canal, Hawaii, Portugal and the final destination of Southampton, England, discovering new lands and people of different nationalities. Our eyes were open in wonderment at the different traditions of each country.

In those days writing letters to our family was a regular fortnightly ritual for me and my mother with the giving and receiving of presents at Christmas and birthdays for the whole family.

Sue and I worked in London and enjoyed our first Christmas with snow, which is something we had not envisaged before. The snowflakes started falling gently outside our flat and two crazy Aussies rushed down three flights of stairs to view the spectacle. It was magic to us and we jumped up and down in delight on the street outside our flat. People started looking out their windows to find out what the commotion was, although this didn't deter our amazement at these tiny little flakes of white atmospheric vapour falling from the sky.

Over the next few days the snow thickened, making it a perfect white Christmas for us to enjoy with a few friends we met from the ship. Six months later after buying a Combi van, a school friend of my sister's joined us on our travels through England, Wales and Scotland. These local towns had many Churches and Cathedrals to view with our eventual conclusion to visit a local pub for a different type of entertainment.

Leaving the snow-covered lands of Scotland where the cold was too much for us to bear, allowed these three young girls to travel over the English Channel to Holland. This visit lasted three months during which the three of us were hired as chambermaids for an American hotel.

The three of us parted ways in Holland as my sister joined the Hari Krishna movement and her friend ventured to Yugoslavia (as it was named then) to visit where her parents were born.

A flat mate from London joined me with the intent to travel through Europe. The Combi van had journeyed to car heaven, leaving our feet to be the leader. We travelled through parts of Belgium and eventually to Paris, although our itchy feet kept us moving towards the countryside of France, eventually flagging down a man in a sports car. He was Flemish which is the Dutch speaking linguistic group constituting 59% of the Belgian population with the French speaking comprising the rest.

This gentle man was travelling alone after losing his wife and child in a car accident. We felt he needed the company and we were both eager to be with him as long as he wished. Our journey ventured through Monaco to Italy with his map of detailed itinerary he wished to view. We were treated to meals, accommodation and his comprehensive knowledge of each town we visited. Eventually this man left us in Rome with a heartfelt thanks to this beautiful human being for his compassion for two travellers.

Unfortunately, that was the end of our travels as my companion wished to travel back to England.

Over the next few years I resided in London with travels to Germany infrequently. My last big travel was to Canada for nearly one year which is elaborated on, in another chapter.

On the day I arrived back in London, heading towards Kensington, my old digs, in the pursuit of claiming my belongings, I noticed a three-storey building named Biba's (the spelling may not be so accurate). As there was a need to powder my nose; if you get my drift, I ventured in and was taken by lift to the third floor. As the doors to the lift opened, there in front of me, was my previous flat mate Victor. What a surprise! I had left the apartment we shared with two others, for an adventure to the unknown, on the other side of the world.

Victor had already introduced me to my future husband when we shared the flat, although at the time, I was seeing someone else. Within a few weeks of seeing Victor again, I met my future husband at a party.

Travelling broadens the mind and educates us on environments, culture and the people on the land which in turn can change our point of view.

The flowing cascades of travel were about to end. A new waterfall of change was about to present itself.

Mothers Are Special

At the beginning of 1974, I realized it was time for me to change the flow of my river and return to my family in Australia. After all, the overseas trip which was originally planned for two years had ended up lasting more than four. At the time, I was living in London with my boyfriend. With a little nudge, he decided to join me on the journey back to Australia.

We flew to Melbourne via Sydney where we stopped over to stay with our friend Victor, who had flown home three months earlier. During our fleeting visit we took in the sights with ferry rides to Manly and Luna Park; Sunday brunch at a seafood café and evening walks to a restaurant or pub in Mosman or Cremorne.

A week later we arrived at my family home without having given any definite arrival details. Sometime before Christmas, I'd said. Knocking on the front door of the family home, I was so excited. Then my mother opened the door. Mum was approximately 172 cms tall, short black hair, olive complexion and greeted me with a surprised, albeit excited, smile on her face.

"Oh! Lynne," she screamed. "Wow! I wasn't expecting you this early." She opened the door and we threw our arms around each other, without comprehending that the screen door had closed in my boyfriend's face. Suddenly realising he wasn't behind me, the door was reopened to introduce my mother to the man I loved.

A young man walked over and said hello but my recognition was blank and promptly thought he might be a neighbour. It was my brother Josh, much taller than when I had left. Dark brown short hair, beautiful blue eyes like our father, a warm smile and a height of 177 cms, which is what Siri said.

I felt so embarrassed. "I'm sorry Josh. You've changed so much I didn't recognise you."

Josh was very understanding and laughed with that friendly smile of his. Realizing later, my change in weight from eating those fish and chips after many late nights out in London, could have given him a fright.

My brother, Brendan's, facial features were exactly the same with short fair hair, except a little older and taller. We also hugged as I introduced my man to everyone. My baby brother Ashley was only six and didn't recognize me. He was very cute with light brown hair and a little shy, hiding behind mum's dress.

"You remember all the letters I read out to you?" Mum asked. "This is your sister, Lynne. She wrote those letters."

Arriving home after a long day working, my father was so excited, running around like a rooster with its head chopped off. Dad had the most beautiful piercing blue eyes and not much taller than mum, although strong and proud. He just had to go to the bottle shop and buy some booze for the fun and celebration which was the night's agenda.

We stayed at the family home for two weeks until we found an apartment in Prahran.

My father suffered a breakdown in January 1975 when he was diagnosed as a manic depressive. This disease was relatively new in the 70's. It has since been renamed bi-polar.

During this time the whole family was worried about my father, without realizing the effect his illness was having on mum. My mother always went about her business in private and no-one knew she was stressed. She had a knack for not showing it.

My mother had a cerebral haemorrhage and died on the 24th September 1975.

Years later when I was receiving a healing, my spirit guide said, "Your mother was worn out and that was why she died."

Mum suffered asthma and bronchitis most of her life. She gave birth to seven children, one of whom died, and suffered two miscarriages.

A week before my mother died, my boyfriend and I were walking down our street with shopping bags in our hands as I caught a glimpse of someone further down the road, which looked like my mother.

I shouted, "Mum is that you?"

She turned around and sure enough, it was my mother. It was out of character for her to visit. On Saturdays, Dad usually went to the footy to watch Richmond (Aussie Rules), the Mighty Tigers, with my younger brothers, repeating the tradition once earmarked to the older sisters. On this particular day Mum decided to visit us and asked Dad to drop her off on his way to the football. Once all the food from our shopping was put away, the three of us proceeded to walk across the road from our apartment, to a little pub never visited. The afternoon was spent reminiscing about my childhood and travels overseas. Mum thought the younger generation's concept of living together before marriage was worth pursuing.

"I would have liked to live with your father before we married."

It was only nine months since returning from overseas and this visit with my mother was the beginning of our getting to know each other again. I was really pleased we hadn't missed her and treasured this time, albeit a short encounter.

A few hours later Dad returned to collect Mum. I hugged her, not knowing that would be the last time I'd see her.

On Monday 21st September, a letter arrived in the mail with a $100 cheque from The Melbourne Cup lottery plus a ticket with a horse's name in the biggest race of the year. This meant if my horse won in the Melbourne Cup, there would be a large sum of money to collect. Picking up the phone and dialling the number to tell my mother about the news, there was hesitation in my voice as my father answered.

"Ah! Hi Dad. Is Mum busy?"

Dad said, "Yes, she's in the kitchen at the moment."

The excitement was running through my veins and I blurted out my news to him.

"Dad I have won $100 and also a ticket with a horse in The Melbourne Cup which means there is a big chance to win again if my horse comes in." He promised to pass my news on to mum.

We talked for a while about his work and then I said goodbye. I never spoke to my mother again.

The 24th September was Show day in Melbourne and a public holiday. This public holiday has since been changed. My boyfriend and I thought about visiting my parents and although it was tempting, we opted for a lazy day together.

That evening there was a knock on the front door and it was my father, looking very upset. He entered the apartment and I promptly poured a brandy with the intention of calming him down.

He said, "I came home from work and found your mother in bed, foaming at the mouth. I talked to the doctor on the phone and he advised me to ring the ambulance, to take her to the hospital. Once we reached the hospital I was asked to leave. Knowing you live a few streets away, I thought I'd come here."

Very shortly after drinking his brandy he insisted on going back to the hospital, promising his return.

Just after my father left, walking into my bedroom, an overwhelming feeling hit me, that my mother would not survive. I believe she died at that moment. The tears welled up in my eyes as I paced up and down the bedroom in disbelief. It seemed like moments later, although it was at least half an hour, when I was interrupted by my father's return. My father and Aunty stood at the door.

Opening the door, I cried out, "She's dead, isn't she?"

My aunty said, "How did you know? We just left the hospital."

I ushered them both in and gave my father another brandy while we deciphered what to do and how to contact the rest of the family.

My sister, Maureen, was working that day and after consulting her superior, we drove to East Bentleigh feeling traumatized by the emotional reaction we all knew was about to play out. Upon our arrival, my father greeted her with the sad news and of course she was extremely upset. I climbed out of the car to comfort her. Mum and Maureen were very close, especially since Sue and I travelled overseas. Eventually climbing back into the car I comforted my little sister during the drive home, where my brothers Ashley and Brendan were waiting, unaware of the tragedy.

My little brother, Ashley, was only six years old. Suddenly I knew his birth was meant to be, even though my mother struggled with the idea of having a child at thirty-nine. Ashley would be there to help my father through this difficult time. Dad would be the sole parent.

Where was Josh? The family sat in the kitchen waiting for him. Finally, he arrived home around 10.30pm. He had been home all day with Mum and around 3pm left to catch up with friends, on her insistence.

"Go out with your friends because your father will be home shortly. I'll just lie down for a while as I have a headache."

It was a terrible time. My mother was only 46. All my plans for us to become re-acquainted vanished, as now it was too late.

A few days later during the church service of her funeral; seated in the front row between Josh and Brendan brought tears to my eyes, witnessing their sadness. Wrapping my arms around their shoulders to comfort them, the mother instinct greeted me. A few days later entangled in a delayed reaction of sobbing in my boyfriend's arms, shock permeated throughout my body and in turn I succumbed to the flu, which lasted many weeks.

In retrospect, my mother visiting me the week before she died, was not a coincidence; (besides I don't believe in coincidence, as I believe certain events occur like a domino effect for each of us to learn) plus deciding not to visit the family home and Josh going out with his mates; subconsciously or consciously, my mother knew she was going to die and she needed to be alone.

After my mother died, her spirit watched over me, so various people led me to believe. At that time in my life, I was oblivious to what they really meant and shrugged my shoulders. Not really understanding the significance of their words but listening anyway.

This waterfall of life shook my heart and sent it spiralling deep into the water below, causing emotional turmoil and disbelief, unable to surface to the mind of understanding. Eventually with time, the cascade starts to flow over a rocky surface.

The river turned into a huge rapid of unknown emotional turmoil.

Changing My Health

Once the rapids of life started to subside, time alone healed the waters of tears and emotion. Suddenly the next progressive change was about to begin.

It took two years after my mother died, for my boyfriend and me to move to Sydney. The house we rented in Mosman was large with three unused rooms at the back, which could be utilized as a separate area with its own entrance. A tall young man with dark hair joined our household for a short time and used these rooms. People are in one's life for a reason and he was in mine to introduce me to another way of dealing with my asthma. He suggested Naturopathy.

After mum died I was very unwell for weeks and wasn't smoking which helped me to comprehend this being an opportunity to stop smoking altogether. After all it was only when socialising that smoking was important, so a distraction was needed. The only obstacle was keeping my fingers occupied and the best therapy for me was knitting. Most of the family received a jumper or scarf and I even knitted myself a pink jacket. Asthma was a part of my life since the age of three and now at 26 my mind was registering more clearly, the effects of smoking on my health. Mum would be proud of me.

On my first visit to the Naturopath she pre-scribed a strict diet of no dairy, red meat or alcohol. The diet was very restricting especially when invited to dinner with friends, as my menu would invariably end up being vegetables and non-alcoholic drinks. Determination spread through my veins enabling me to continue. Grains were a great substitute for protein although preparing them was difficult for me as somehow the pot always ended up burnt. Being very active moving from one activity to another and very rarely sitting still caused me to forget the pot that was boiling, hence a burnt one. The third attempt caused me to throw my hands in the air, disillusioned. During this time anaemia spread through my body with the lack of protein and iron. My Naturopath suggested eating liver which was adequate for a short time, except it wasn't my favourite food. In time, fish and chicken were substituted with the occasional vegetarian meal.

Because of the changed diet and regular acupuncture treatments, the usual intake of approximately 100 asthma tablets in one year, was reduced to three. The side effects of taking these tablets would result in my hands shaking and heart palpitations. The reduction of these tablets was a mind-blowing improvement. Keeping strictly to my diet produced astounding results. During this time, I was introduced to a Ventolin spray by my Doctor, which wasn't as aggressive to the body with faster results. This spray was always in my handbag and used when needed.

Opportunities come to us in different ways. Our tenant convinced me to make an appointment with his Naturopath; changing my health considerably. This traditional natural therapy treatment is part of my healthy life today. It is my way of dealing with a health issue; that worked for me.

The cascade is flowing healthily along to greet the next fork in the journey.

In my next book, you will discover what caused my asthma.

Counselling – Past Life Experiences

The cascade of flowing water twists and turns in different directions and sometimes surprises the unsuspecting stream of life.

From time to time I would attend a massage course to improve my skills as a Beauty Therapist. During one such massage course, the facilitator encouraged me to attend a counselling session. These sessions sent me on another discovery tour of alternative therapies, which instigated my travelling back in time to several past lives. My belief is that some of those past lives were presented for my resolution, in this life time. The culmination of each past life has given me a series of life lessons that eventually brought me to a certain point in my life. The significance of these lives has been established in future chapters and my second book.

Around 1990, I attended a massage course facilitated by a tall, slim redheaded woman and I'm guessing, in her forties. At the end of my third class she beckoned me to her side.

"I feel from my observation that you are going through a great deal of stress in your life and I may be able to help you. I am also a counsellor. Here is my card."

Taking the card and thanking her I thought to myself... that was very astute of her, as I was thinking of leaving my husband. The following day, rummaging through my bag, I found the business card and without much thought, picked up the phone to make an appointment.

A week later with excitement in my bones by this new venture, an ounce of trepidation crept in. Arriving late was a cardinal sin, especially for professional appointments and yet here I was scrutinizing the map because of losing my way. In those days mobile phones weren't as popular an item, as they are now.

Finally arriving 10 minutes late, this tall redhead reassured me by saying, "When people are late, it's often a sign they are subconsciously unsure about counselling. Follow me to the treatment room."

The room consisted of a table with two chairs and a massage table adjacent. The antique furniture blended in with the dark maroon curtains, giving the room a gypsy-like appearance.

Sitting on one of the chairs provided, my body began to relax. The Counsellor sat opposite and proceeded to ask the preliminary questions about my background, before venturing to query the reason for my visit. During that discussion, my marriage was the main topic.

My decision over the preceding days had been to stay with my husband, because I still loved him. We discussed our situation for hours, prior to the counselling session and ironed out some of our difficulties. Unequivocally this was the right decision, I thought. My presumption was that the counselling would help me understand any reservations I may have about staying in the marriage.

Two weeks later feeling more in control and arriving early for my second session, a smile was my greeting. Promptly she escorted me to another treatment room where I sat waiting for her to begin. This time when she sat down in front of me, I noticed in her hand, a box of tiny little bottles.

The method was called aura soma. "Can you pick out each bottle separately and take in the smell. Put aside the bottle that uplifts you and secondly the one that disturbs you."

I did as she requested and chose the two opposing bottles of liquid, presenting them in front of her.

"Can you alternate smelling the two bottles and pick out the one you feel drawn to?"

After choosing a bottle I lay down on the massage table and was covered with a blanket.

"How are you feeling?"

"Fine," I said, not knowing how I was supposed to be feeling.

"Can you feel or see anything?"

"I can see visions of people." I then journeyed back to a past life.

This was my first initiation to past live therapy.

The vision was of me as a small child around 7 years old in London, England, caught stealing a loaf of bread. I was thrown in jail, alone; in a room that was dark and dingy. During my confinement in this jail, because of the lack of sustenance, my body became extremely thin and bony; undoubtedly on my way to death. The lack of nourishment contributed to my weakness. During my stay, rats would come and go, obviously drawn to my condition. Before too long I suffered the rats eating me, a defenceless child, too weak to defend myself. I felt the pain of being eaten which instigated my death.

I was very disturbed by this event as my mind returned to the room. After feeling more present, the Counsellor gestured to move to another room where she presented me with a cup of tea and something to eat.

She looked at me with enquiring eyes, "Are you alright?"

I muttered, "yes" without consulting my body first, which was in a state of shock and disbelief. I ate furiously and drank the cup of tea which helped to bring my body back to its normal realism.

She took over the situation by advocating, "I suggest you have another appointment in two weeks' time, to allow your body to assimilate and understand today's outcomes. When you are feeling comfortable to leave and drive home, I will show you out."

After a short time, my body felt secure to drive home, nevertheless my mind was questioning this experience. During the next two weeks I tried hopelessly to eradicate my memories of that encounter. My body was trying desperately to assimilate and understand what actually happened through my mind's eye.

* * *

Two weeks later arriving for my third appointment on time, I was intrigued by this process of past life genre. Being taken to the room and offered the same bottles from the last appointment to smell, gave me a sense of reassurance which kept me captivated. After smelling the bottles and making my choice I lay on the massage table. Again, my mind wandered back to a past life. The experience was like dreaming with coloured pictures, of the events in my past life history. As the events appeared in my mind I explained these visions. It was like being on centre stage of a movie, so to speak. I only saw snippets of the whole picture.

In this past life, I was a man. It was during a war (being a novice at this past life stuff, I did not ask which war and what year). There were many prisoners and my superior ordered me to cut off their heads with a sword. I protested. My superior said it was an order or my head would go instead. Regrettably I killed many men with the sword. It reminded me of the Hitler era, but I think it was many hundreds of years before. More like one of the Japanese wars. I was mortified having witnessed these horrific deeds. Feeling sick and extremely angry at committing such atrocities, my body very quickly emerged from this session suffering extreme trauma. There was justification for my behaviour being self-preservation; a life or death situation. Someone else would have been ordered to perform the deed if not me, although at the same time, there was disbelief of myself committing such deeds.

Again, the process of eating and drinking to allow the body to be grounded was completed, before being released from this traumatic event.

* * *

A young man was introduced to me at my fourth session of this past life exploration.

My vision was of a young man, who was a soldier in the cavalry, at war with the Indians in America. An Indian Chief speared the arrow which was lodged in my back and left me to die. The dry hot day very quickly turned into night, bringing to mind the scavenger dogs that would approach upon smelling my blood. Luckily before the dogs appeared, a man travelling past rescued me back to his log cabin. The man and his wife treated the wound but knew a doctor was needed. Within minutes the man went in search of a doctor, leaving his wife to care for me.

Unfortunately, it was too late when the man returned with the doctor, as I died soon afterwards. The feeling of pain from my wounds was quite severe; then suddenly upon death there was peace with no pain. Witnessing my spirit floating out of my body to view the scene below of the three individuals crouched around my body, heralded an epiphany.

My mind was prompted to return to the room where the treatment was taking place. Slowly feeling in control, there was this knowledge of experiencing something really incredible. To me this unquestionably answered many theories of, "What happens when we die? When we die our spirit lives on and we float or travel to a more peaceful existence. The pain from my wounds precipitated my death; however after the release of this pain there was complete freedom, as my spirit floated out of my body."

* * *

My fifth session heralded a slight change as my vision on travelling back was of a girl. At the age of eight my father died and my mother and I were ostracized from the village because we had no means of support. Eventually the village mayor, who lived in a huge house, procured me from my mother. The house was surrounded by a high fence made of steel rods with spears attached to the ends at the highest point. The mayor was my master and he gave me the job of cleaning his home.

After one year, my master allowed me to see my mother. We spent a beautiful day together, although not knowing when I would see her again.

The task that morning before visiting my mother was to clean a large carpet. On my return the master told me to clean the carpet again as it was dirty.

My protest was ignored so I decided to run away. The fence surrounding the house looked so fierce and extremely high that it was impossible to climb, notwithstanding the result of me being severely cut by the sharp spears at the top. I waited behind the columns outside the house, planning my escape. Suddenly I heard voices close by and there was nothing else to do but run. My master caught sight of me and took chase. He threw the long sword in his hand and my left arm was cut off. I was stopped in my tracks and lay on the ground bleeding profusely. I died very quickly from the loss of blood. Again, my soul left my body and my spirit was looking down on the scene below. I could see my master looking very sad, as he said that he only wanted to stop me, not to kill me.

This past life involving my arm has reappeared in this life time with unusual circumstances and astounding results. It appears in the chapter, "Pain in my Arm."

After each session I was quite traumatized. Most of my sessions were held a few hours before collecting my son from school. So upon reflection, my body was still very much in shock. On one occasion walking from my car to the school yard, another parent approached me.

"Lynne, you look like you have seen a ghost. Are you ok?"

"Yes, I have just finished a counselling session and drove straight here to the school."

Until that comment was made I was oblivious to the extent this counselling was affecting me.

My fascination with these past lives led me to blurt out my experiences in conversation with other mums from the school. Some mothers seemed relaxed with my stories, on the other hand others thought me to be quite weird. Realizing my inappropriateness of discussing this concept to these individuals, I promptly stopped.

Years later upon mentioning these stories to different individuals the response was enthusiastic. I was speaking to the initiated and those who were willing to listen, even if they didn't understand. Wow! This was all new to me as well.

My sixth session was a huge experience.

In this past life in the sixteenth century, I was a young girl living somewhere in Sicily during the Sicilian and Spanish Great War. I was an only child. My father was appointed by the King as a General, commanding the army which instigated him being away at war most of the time. My parents and I lived with the King and Queen in separate quarters of the castle.

As my mother entertained on many occasions to alleviate her boredom, she left me to my own devices. I was bored being left alone by myself. My mother saw this and decided to hold a big birthday party for me and invite some children around my age.

At the party there was an elephant decorated in bright colours for all the children to ride on. It was great having a party and riding on the elephant however I was not used to all these children and hid myself away in a corner.

Surveying the scene, I noticed a boy standing alone and decided to go and talk to him. His name was Roberto and from then on we became very close friends. A few years later we married. One year after marrying Roberto, I gave birth to a son named Antonio.

Roberto was a soldier and he travelled with my father to war. He was normally away for three months at a time and when he returned he stayed for around the same time.

One very tragic day my father returned home to tell me that my husband was killed in battle. Unable to control my emotion, I ran to my room. My body was completely frozen with sorrow, nevertheless unable to shed tears.

From that moment on I carried on with life as if the death of my husband was put behind me. My brave face was shown to the public, although whenever alone I mourned for my husband without ever crying. This facade was maintained by me for many years. No-one knew, or if they did no-one said anything.

When he was about twelve years old my son married and thence had two children. My mother decided that I needed to remarry. She started to introduce me to prospective suitors. Finally, after some time, my mother suggested a man named Johnno whom I thought was suitable and we were married.

However, after a very short time, I committed suicide by taking a potion. After dying, my spirit left my body and I saw myself looking down on the scene. My vision was of family members and friends who were very distraught, not understanding why I had taken my life.

After marrying Johnno, my realization was, that I wasn't worthy of him. I was still very much in love with my first husband and had not forgotten him. For this reason, I could not give myself completely to Johnno and felt unworthy of my new husband, so the decision was made, to be with my first husband in heaven.

I screamed while these events unfolded in my session and thought…"what have I done?" This was a real tragedy. It took me a while to come to terms with what I had just witnessed in this past life.

A little while after that session I realized that my husband in this life was the reincarnation of that second husband. My immediate thought was, "I must make amends for committing suicide and stay with him in this life." Somehow a karmic revelation would happen. Those were my thoughts…then.

I didn't have any more past life sessions. This surge of adrenalin from each session was a definite torrent of the waters rushing towards the waterfall edge plunging down to the unknown depths of emotion. In the end there was a sign of excitement as these lives unfolded, giving a unique view of life and death.

Persistent Dream

During the next few years the ripple of a cascade had taken shape over the rocks calming the waters. Although what lay ahead was an outpouring of rough waters.

This incident taught me that if there is a problem in our lives which isn't resolved, it will bite us on the bum and return. It is recognised that in our 40s we can have a midlife crisis. Well this was mine. The resurrection of the past instigated an introduction to kinesiology and a life changing direction.

Around February/March in 1994 I started having the same dream about an incident that occurred in 1973 while living overseas. The dream persisted every night for a couple of weeks. On reflection, this consistent dream was a significant part of my life and maybe counselling would finally release the issue. Counselling had never been offered at the time of the incident, however many years later when consulting counsellors on other issues, this subject never transpired.

My decision was to contact a friend from the meditation group I attended and convey my concerns of this consistent dream, whereupon she suggested seeing a kinesiologist and promptly recommended the appropriate people to call.

I telephoned one of the names on the list for an appointment. She was in the process of moving overseas but was able to fit me in before she departed Australia.

Arriving at the address the next day I found myself in a luxury apartment block and sceptically knocked on the door. The door opened and I was greeted by a young girl with long black hair pulled back in a ponytail, revealing her youthful looks. She showed me to a small consulting room and suggested sitting in the seat provided as she sat opposite. With pen in hand my particulars were written down plus an explanation for the visit.

During my account of the recurring dream, a steady flow of tears rolled over my cheeks causing make-up to run down my face and more than likely, the beginnings of a smudged clown face.

The dreams were about an incident that occurred during my travels overseas. No-one knew about this part of my life except my overseas friends left behind and my boyfriend. Over the past 23 years whenever someone talked about rape or there was a movie on the subject my feet quickly exited the room. There was never any information given at the time of the incident, on how to deal with this situation.

My memories were of having an exceptional time through meeting a group of amazing single parents from both sexes. We shared many good times together at parties, dinners and especially surprise birthday celebrations. The informal group welcomed me with open arms. Amongst the group were a few single souls as myself, which was very reassuring.

Whoever was given a surprise party for their birthday never realised until the event. They had a knack of being able to conceal it from the unsuspecting individual.

I lived in a bedsit a few streets away from my friend and her son. This was the first person that befriended me and introduced me to the group. The bedsit was my home although only ever used to sleep and shower. I was always out working or playing as living alone was not my usual lifestyle, more than likely because of being raised in a family of six children.

During my stay at the bedsit I met this tall, good looking Capricorn with beautiful brown eyes. He shared a two-bedroom apartment with four guys. We gelled straight away. A few weeks after seeing him on a regular basis, he informed me that he and his buddies had found a house on the north side of town.

"Would you like to join me when the boys and I move into the house?"

I said, "Yes, fabulous!" The bedsit had definitely gone past its use by date, plus I really liked this guy. He informed me much later that he didn't think I would say yes.

The six of us moved into the house. It was fun at first but a little overwhelming at being the only girl and him being the only male with a girlfriend. I was 23 and he was 19. Surprisingly, younger men were always attracted to me and still are many years later.

One night the boys went out and he didn't come home. The next day he made up some feeble excuse about why he didn't come home. As you can imagine I wasn't happy.

A couple of weeks later a friend invited me to one of those surprise parties. My boyfriend declined the invitation and the bus was my option for transport. The party was fun, as I knew most of the people in addition to being a little stoned.

It was suggested to stay the night, although taking note of what transpired at home, two weeks previous, my decision was to hitch a ride home.

The rest of this written word is about the true story of my dream, relayed to my Kinesiologist:

I was hitching on the main road from the party and managed to hail a driver who was travelling as far as the city area. Approaching the city he stopped and while getting out of the car, another car stopped immediately beside me.

The driver of the second vehicle yelled out, "Do you want a lift?"

My initial thought was – "No! Don't get into this car." Stupidly, I dismissed this thought, anxious to get home.

The driver asked me, "Where are you going?"

"To Main Street"

This was the closest street to my home although far enough away for him not to know the exact location. My intuition was wary of this man.

Eventually in Main Street, I suggested to the driver, "This will be far enough."

He immediately stopped the car to let me out. Opening the door and sliding out of the seat, I thanked him.

Before having a chance to walk away he said, "You better get back in the car."

Turning my head to look around, what confronted me was a gun pointing straight at me. Unflinchingly, I sat straight down on the seat. He told me to lie down underneath the seat and then drove for about 15 minutes.

While I trembled under the seat my mind was racing. Was he going to kill me? What would he do with me? What could I do? How could I get out of this situation?

Finally, he stopped the car and let me sit up. I was sweating and scared. Surveying the scene, I noticed we were in an industrial estate of some kind. Opening his car door, he hopped out and walked around the estate with his gun in hand. Returning to the car he grabbed the door and placed the gun on the dashboard while sitting in his seat. Suddenly he jumped out of the car and walked around the perimeter.

While sitting there my mind triggered many thoughts, such as picking up the gun and shooting him, except never having used a gun before, what would the consequences be? Would that really help me? Being uneducated on the use or handling of guns would render him able to retrieve the gun relatively easily. Aiming the gun to shoot, then killing him in the attempt would make me a killer. The police would not accept my plea of self-defence.

As these thoughts were going through my mind, he opened my door and pushed me over to the driver's seat. He grabbed the gun and asked me to undress slowly. It was all a game to him, a power game. I slowly undressed. He put the gun down and performed his sickly game with me not looking at him and closing my eyes as much as possible. I could have fought and screamed but he had a gun and no-one was around for miles.

Whilst dressing after the ordeal was over, my mind started thinking about my retribution. He drove me back to my original destination. My decision was to walk to the back of the car, memorize his number plate, and give it to the police. Running home, my mind was on the reception waiting for me.

On my arrival, the boys were watching TV, looking very stoned. I quickly grabbed a piece of paper and wrote down the details of the number plate. My boyfriend noticed me and walked out of the room.

"How was the party?" he said.

With my voice cracking and the tears starting to flow, I proceeded to convey the events of the night.

"I want to call the police to give them the number plate details." He said, "You need to calm down and get some sleep."

I was surprised at his statement but wasn't in a fit state to argue and did as requested. He cuddled me all night.

In the morning, my friend rang to make sure I arrived home safely. Articulating my story, she became very angry knowing that the incident wasn't reported.

"Make sure you are ready as I will take you to the police station myself. I'll be there in half an hour to pick you up."

Half an hour later she arrived. I quickly raced out to the car so there was no confrontation.

At the police station, I was ushered into a room with a policeman and asked to relay the whole story. It was very embarrassing telling a stranger all the gory events in detail. He then gave me a notepad to write down my interpretation in writing. This made me feel like a criminal.

The policeman took me to another room where an examination was performed by a nurse, although that was my presumption as I wasn't informed. The clothes that were worn the night before were taken from me as evidence. It was my favourite light green suit and was never returned to me. The police suggested staying in town which made me feel they didn't believe a word spoken.

Days later the police phoned to inform me that my evidence had helped them find the car in question. The owner of the car was charged with having an unregistered gun. He told the police he thought I was a prostitute.

A few months later, not having heard anything from the police, I rang to inform them of my return to England. The police were adamant for me to wait for the trial. Nevertheless, that could take years and my immediate requirement was returning to England to claim my belongings, left behind at a friend's house. I also didn't relish the thought of standing up in court reliving the gory details of the rape. How humiliating. I was never offered any counselling.

Now here I was telling the Kinesiologist about my dream, reliving a memory of something that happened to me 23 years before.

She asked me to stand up and hold my hands out in front of me with my palms up. She then asked my body for permission to release this pain. Once permission was granted she proceeded to ask relevant questions pertaining to the event. This technique was quite intriguing as I hadn't experienced it before. Her mission was to remove the pain from my body through muscle testing with the help of my spirit.

After she had removed all the pain she asked, "How are you feeling?"

"I am surprised by my answer, because I am actually more concerned about the way the police treated me, than the rapist. I felt dirty and unwanted when returning home to my boyfriend. The police made me feel like the guilty person who had committed a crime. There was no compassion for the innocent party after going through such a traumatic experience. Because of my unclean feeling the only escape was to leave the household."

"How would you have liked to be treated during that time?"

"I would have liked to be believed or at least heard before being judged guilty. I would have liked to feel clean and not dirty. It was something I had no control over."

"Take your mind back to the year when you were twenty-three and take your feelings right now with you. How do you feel right now about the incident?"

"I feel okay. It doesn't seem as huge as I always thought."

"I am going to bring you through your life from age twenty-three until today, to make sure your body has released this pain."

Taking me through my years of 23, 28, 30, 35, 40, and finally 46, she made sure I was comfortable with the incident at each of those years.

At each age, I acknowledged my true feelings. "I am comfortable and not fearful anymore."

When the session finished, she said, "If you need another appointment it will have to be in the next week, as I am leaving for overseas. But I don't think you will. However, if something else arises after I have left, here are some phone numbers of people you may wish to contact."

"Thank you. I feel so much lighter in my body, it's almost like I have lost weight." I had actually lost that traumatic dark energy which gave me the feeling of being slimmer.

"If the body is ready to receive healing then one session is all that is needed."

This was exactly the case for me. The recurring dreams of the incident meant that my body was ready to heal and let it go.

Days after the counselling, my lips imparted the story to friends which was never possible beforehand. My whole demeanour changed as the scared and dirty feelings disappeared, making the incident minuscule.

* * *

Two weeks later flicking the remote from one station to another the movie, "The Accused" starring Jodie Foster flashed in front of me. Having no idea about the content, I decided to watch it. In the movie, Jodie's character was gang raped which made me extremely angry. However, the character procured justice which pleased me immensely resulting in never watching another movie in that genre.

The feeling of satisfaction and honour came to mind when reliving the Kinesiology experience. Reliving this story enabled a change of energy in my body and psyche. Unbeknown to me at the time, this unravelling of a major incident was the start of my personal healing.

This explosion of troubled waters was relived to change the turmoil experienced throughout the body, releasing the haunted suffering to bring the rainstorm back to a peaceful healing cascade.

Leaving My Marriage

The release of the deep-seated turbulence of a past event created smoothness in the waters, for the time being.

This chapter clarifies what transpired after the release of the traumatic event, relived, in the persistent dreams of the previous chapter.

Not long after this counselling session, the family travelled by plane to Melbourne for Easter. We stayed in Cheltenham with friends, only a five minute walk to the station with trains arriving every 15 minutes. Using public transport was a novelty as we usually travelled by car when visiting Melbourne.

I enjoyed the early morning walks on the beach, taking in the crisp blue sea while the sun was rising in the distance. This time, together with the sand in my feet and the smell of the clean fresh air, helped me to unwind. Putting one's feet in the water and swimming at the beach are a beautiful way of washing all the old stale energy from one's body. I felt rejuvenated again and happy when it was time to return home.

A few weeks after our Easter break, I was back into the normal routine of running my beauty business and attending a meditation class every second Friday night. The Friday after returning from Melbourne was the scheduled class. There were usually around five or six women and sometimes a guy. The class was held in a friend's house, around 7.30pm and we finished with refreshments.

On this evening during my meditation, a spirit presence appeared in front of me and communicated this message, "It is time to leave your marriage. Both of you have achieved the lessons you needed from this relationship and it is time to move on. You have achieved a higher spiritual connection than your husband and he won't be able to catch up."

My reaction was a horrified protest after which the spirit disappeared and left me to decipher the magnitude of this statement. My mind was racing. "How could a spirit suggest this?" Marriage was forever, even though happiness had escaped my soul. During this altercation with self, our facilitator suggested slowly coming back to the room, abandoning the meditative state. Still trying to understand this phenomenon, my solution was not to reveal any particulars at this time.

Meditation is helping to clear the mind of the everyday activities and being with oneself. It's like a holiday from life, although through the mind. The whole body is relaxed as well, which gives one clearer and more positive thoughts. My mind sometimes goes back to past lives and I talk to the spirits of the dead. Quite often messages are received which help me achieve my goals.

A couple of years earlier confiding my feelings about my marriage to a good friend, she suggested joining her meditation group for some clarity. Meditation was suggested to me on other occasions, although life seemed to take over.

My first taste of meditation was in Sydney in a yoga class where half an hour was allocated for meditation following the primary class. I always found it hard to clear my head from the little voices talking all the time: where was I going? What time was that appointment? Who made that comment or what shall I cook for dinner? My mind never seemed to stop talking. I thoroughly enjoyed the class because even though my mind was active, my body did relax. Our teacher was from New Zealand and she knew exactly how to explain and demonstrate the movements of yoga as well as how to help our minds to relax. During that year my mind started to wind down.

Meditation was also suggested to me when travelling overseas in the 70's; however, I was moving around too much to be able to start a class.

Very soon after starting these classes there was a distinct feeling of smelling the roses, so to speak. Being tied up with my own problems, there was no room for the other joys in life.

Three months after that meditation class, waking from sleep, sitting up straight, looking into space, I suddenly realized it was time to leave my marriage. Stagnation was setting in and without moving on I would die inside. This meant my disclosure of the intention of leaving was imminent. The timing wasn't right as his mother had just returned to England, after spending six weeks holiday with our family. When is a good time anyway? He didn't think I was serious, having tried to leave twice before and returned.

This time my decision was absolute giving me renewed energy to find suitable accommodation for myself and the children. After looking for a short time and viewing a four bedroom house with a pool, my decision was made. The pool would keep the children occupied, especially if their friends visited. My son only stayed for a few weeks. He was angry with me and he felt sorry for his father alone in the house. As a result he moved back with him. Stopping him was futile; he was thirteen and didn't need any more conflict in his life; besides he could end up hating me if I interfered. My belief was that boys needed quality time with their fathers during their teenage years. It was better to lose him for a short time now, knowing he would see me fortnightly on weekends. It was hard to endure, although he would gain great strength from his own decision being played out. We now have a great love and respect for each other.

A few weeks after leaving my marriage, I realised this was my solution to rectify the 16th century past life mistake, of committing suicide. This life's option was to leave the marriage and not take my life, allowing me to enjoy many years of happiness, love and learning. To me this meant that my karmic debt was fulfilled.

The river of life came out of turmoil into tranquil waters for a short time, then transcended to the heights of excitement and unfamiliar circumstances. Thus, creating change in the direction of the cascade to give new focus on life.

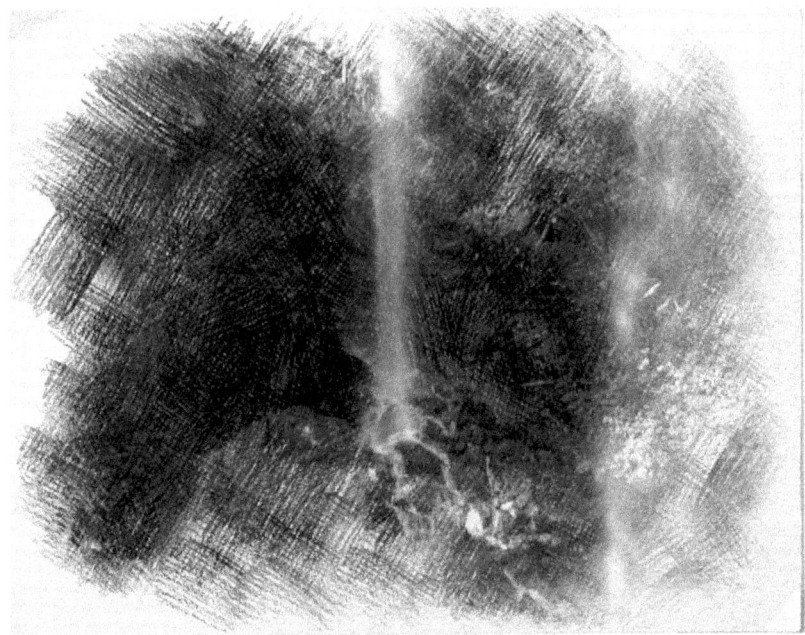

How I dealt with Depression

Depression affects people in many ways, tormenting the mind, similar to a deluge of swollen rivers running at a powerful pace, unable to stop to consider the best way to deal with the situation. This is my way of handling a sensitive conundrum.

In August 1996, one year after leaving my marriage, my business closed which meant the only solution was to set up a room to work from home. August seems to be the month of the year that I experience great change. My father, my rock, was unwell and with him living in Melbourne, made it hard for me to be with him.

In November, my world turned topsy-turvy. I experienced the worst case of depression in my existence. My usual response to being down was switching on the stereo and listening to music, thus soothing the soul. The right music would get my toes tapping and my feet dancing in no time. Whatever brought on the anxious energy would disappear within a short time and the next day the incident was erased from the mind.

This occasion was very different. My car was sitting in the driveway after many repairs having taken place over the past few months. It needed more repairs and I wasn't willing to throw money down the drain any more so it sat there. Eventually my solution was to give the car to my mechanic, who could make good use of the new tyres and other parts. My neighbours offered to take my daughter to and from school as their children attended the same school. I was grateful for this because there was no public transport and it was too far to walk. Once she left for school, my routine was to stare at the walls for hours or go back to bed for the rest of the day, only dragging myself out around 2pm, showering and dressing in time for her return. My brave face hid the real feeling of dying inside.

Treatments to clients were performed with ease giving my body a reprieve from the immediate situation, although as soon as they disappeared the bed beckoned me back. This behaviour continued for six weeks before it occurred to me something was fundamentally wrong. Directing me to little projects of housework or grocery shopping provided no relief.

My internal body had shut down in shock, leaving the external body to react like a robot performing tasks as needed to be executed. What was happening to me? Why did this happen? Was I going through a breakdown? I was finally questioning my state of health.

Retracing my memory made me realize the significance of three events that happened within one week, in early November. The three events were: the loss of my car, my workload diminishing and dismissing a man from my life. On recollection three months before these events, there was the loss of my business and one year previous, my marriage evaporated. These contributing factors caused my body to malfunction.

When my business closed, my flat mate couldn't fathom how I kept going. His response was, "most men would fall apart if they lost their business." It was an enervating experience to be in, although one cannot give up and die. Working from home for the time being was my only solution. Well, until I could come up with another resolution.

My usually positive spirit retreated deep inside, unable to comprehend the affect these incidents were having on my physical being. Inadvertently the depression was telling me something was amiss because happiness and joy practically disappeared from my life. It was up to me to decipher why this depression was having an adverse effect on me. Once the realization slapped me in the face, it was time to take action and resolve it, making the road to recovery much easier.

Having established this situation was mind-blowing with the next step to heal and grow from this experience. If anything negative happens to me, the first response is to experience the pain or anguish and then look at what this incident is teaching. When my business closed suddenly there was a lot of trauma associated with this event. Eventually after a long hard look at me, the realization struck a deep cord. I was whisked out of that situation because there was a need for me to heal myself, which would then enable me to heal others. Hence, where I am now is healing others and teaching them to heal through loving themselves and meditation.

Understanding why the depression took hold of me was the first crucial step to begin the healing process. Now is the time to feel good about myself. After all, this was really another one of life's lessons. At various times in my life I have wondered, "when are these lessons going to end." Once one has inhaled the situation and understood the lesson being taught, then there is a reprieve and life runs smoother. If we are not learning all the time, there is no need for us to be here on earth.

Being isolated at home, running a business and living in the same area, was not the best situation for me, at that time. I realised my friends hadn't contacted me, which meant recapturing my soul was up to me. The plan was finding suitable premises to conduct my services, within a close distance because of transport.

During this time my search was in the career section of the newspaper, for any positions or premises available. At the beginning of January there was an advertisement for a beauty therapist to work in a hairdressing salon with my own separate entrance. As the position was close to home and commencement was the end of January, this was perfect.

The frequency of the bouts of depression became less during the following months, allowing me to feel happy within myself, once more. Whenever I felt the feelings reappear, it was time to make myself laugh or treat myself. To this day, I have not felt any feelings of depression. Recognising the cause of my depression helped me to decipher the ultimate solution.

We need to be kind to ourselves whenever these seemingly disastrous events appear, regardless if it takes days, months or years. Do something that brings a smile to your face. Keep giving love to others and that love will come back to you. Treat yourself as you would like others to treat you, with forgiveness and love.

In retrospect, just after leaving my husband, I attended an osteopath appointment, and she suggested the need for me to have a holiday. I ignored this suggestion because of time and money. Time away from one's situation will change the energy to be able to deal with the immediate state of affairs.

As long as we learn from each situation; this is life's voyage.

Once the treacherous rivers subsided and the waterfall slowed its pace, stillness was created, allowing the river to run at its normal pace.

My Father

This river flowed with special meaning as a parent, although there were stormy waters with this being one of the roughest.

Sometime in February 1998 I rang my father to advise him I would not be able to visit Melbourne for his 70th birthday.

As a single mother, my decision was to work part-time which enabled me to be home more frequently for my daughter, who was nine. This meant flying to Melbourne was not possible.

Ten years previously Brendan and I verbalized to father that regrettably we would not be able to attend his 60th birthday bash, giving him our various reasons. But unbeknown to him we planned a surprise; without our father's knowledge, we decided to travel down together.

My daughter was only six months old and still being fed by the breast. Nevertheless it was important for me to be there. Taking the bus to Sydney with a mini bassinette and having a vacant seat next to me was such a relief as there was more room to manoeuver myself and baby. The lights from the oncoming traffic glaring in my face, including the bus stopping constantly for pick up and drop off, didn't allow for much sleep. That trip changed my perception of travelling by interstate bus forever.

Brendan met me at the bus terminal in Sydney and we transferred all my belongings, including the bassinette into the back seat. This was a much more comfortable journey and safer as the bassinette was strapped up with the seat belt. I was able to relax as she slept nearly all the trip. Brendan insisted on driving all the distance and we stopped only a few times for drink/food/toilet breaks. We caught up with our deep and meaningful philosophies in between a few catnaps for me.

Arriving in Melbourne we drove straight to our Aunties which we previously arranged, to take care of baby for a few hours. Shortly afterwards we jumped into the car heading towards the restaurant.

Brendan drove all the way from Sydney, yet we managed to arrive at the restaurant before anyone else. That was exactly how we wanted it. When Dad appeared he was thrilled and enormously excited. It was worth the journey just to see his face light up.

That experience was ten years ago. This time it was his 70th birthday and my concern was not being there for this special event.

Dad said, "Don't worry; I'll see you at my 80th."

"Of course," but my intuition knew better, as he would not live that long, although my thoughts were never mentioned.

Within a few days of speaking with Dad, it was my usual meditation class on Friday night. During this meditation, a spirit spoke to me.

The spirit said, "You won't be going to your father's 80th birthday because he will die of a heart attack within the next two years."

The spirit continued, "Ask your father for his thoughts about death and what he thinks happens when one dies." After a moment the spirit declared, "Talk to him about death and explain what will happen when he dies."

My body, still in shock once the meditation was finished, took some time to ground. Once it was my time to divulge my experience, this message was not mentioned. The message was given to me for a reason and my prediction that he would not reach 80 was being confirmed although maybe sooner than earlier thought. My father was not in the best of health and my mind was racing on how to bring up this subject.

When ringing my father to wish him a happy birthday, my instinct warned me, this subject was inappropriate at the moment.

A couple of months later, I picked up the phone for a chat with Dad, wondering at the same time how to approach this delicate subject. The fundamental rule is: "Never speak to individuals, especially family, about politics or religion."

As he answered I said, "Hi Dad, it's me Lynne. How are you?"

Dad said, "Fit as a Mallee bull," which was his normal reply.

From his slurred response my feeling was this could be tricky as he undoubtedly was drinking alcohol. After catching up with life's hiccups, I broached the subject.

"Dad, what are your thoughts on death and what happens to us when we die?"

He declared, "I don't know. Besides I'm healthy and have no intention of dying. I'm as fit as a Mallee bull and twice as dangerous. Since the heart bypass I have so much energy."

He made me laugh because he always quoted this colloquialism about the "Mallee bull" when I was growing up. Pursuing the subject was hopeless as his response was the same, referring to his health. Not wanting to harp on the subject, my chat reverted to other topics. My father was never a religious man. He was sent to a religious home in a township outside Sydney when he was eight, along with other siblings. His mother died giving birth to his youngest sister. There were eight children in the family and his father couldn't look after the younger children and work the farm, so six of the children were sent to Sydney. From the stories expressed through my father and his sister, they were treated severely in the so-called religious home. My father was a hard worker and never wanted his children to experience the same wrath as he had endured for five years.

A few weeks later in communication with my father he gave me the same response.

"I'm as fit as a Mallee bull and you'll be coming to my 80th birthday."

My instincts suggested that he would not make it to his 80th birthday. I didn't want to upset him and dropped the subject. There was never another opportunity without upsetting him, to see or speak to him, until his hospitalization in July 1999.

On Tuesday 12th July 1999 at 1am, the phone woke me. It was my brother Brendan. Dad was in hospital. He had suffered a stroke and heart attack which resulted in him being connected to life support. Brendan needed my permission to take Dad off this support, which could mean he would die soon afterwards; not allowing me to see him before his passing.

My mind was racing with thoughts and then eventually I said to Brendan, "I will book a plane to Melbourne today."

After putting the phone down, my feet automatically paced up and down the lounge room floor for about half an hour, without knowing what to do as the shock was taking over my body. My mind kept thinking about last Christmas when father was invited to visit me in Queensland, to allow him to see his grandchildren.

Travelling to Melbourne would mean only seeing me as my finances couldn't stretch to three fares; subsequently suggesting paying for his ticket. He rang one week before Christmas to say money was tight and he wouldn't be coming. He was a proud man. Disappointment clouded my vision temporarily, especially for the children. My father's manic depression or bi-polar was more severe, and when speaking with Brendan it was his belief that Dad should not be on a plane by himself, so I understood.

My sister Sue, who lived in Darwin, had travelled around Australia earlier this year and visited my father and other members of the family. My youngest brother Ashley, who lived in Sydney, had visited Dad as well. The rest of the family lived in Melbourne. My concern was he would die before I saw him. We spoke often on the phone although I was the only sibling unable to see him this year. Pacing backwards and forwards with these thoughts in my head, instinctively the decision was made to go back to bed and sleep, with only a few hours of darkness before endeavouring to organize my trip.

Just before falling asleep my father's voice echoed in my room, he was calling my name.

He said, "Lynne ……..Lynne…………Lynne."

Hearing my name called gave me the confidence that father was going to wait for me, drifting off to sleep reassured. Waking in the morning, my reassurance was still feasible; save for my apprehension of the aftermath.

My first priority was to organize somewhere for my daughter to stay and the best option was with a school friend she was comfortable with. She was happy to be with her friend.

Realizing my next goal was to arrange my flight and knowing the shock was slowly filtering into my body making me incapable of speaking coherently, I telephoned a friend to ask if she would organize a flight to Melbourne later that morning.

An hour later, realizing my body was in slow motion making it impossible for me to make the flight, my phone rang and it was another friend. Trying to communicate to her was difficult enough although she accepted being able to change the flight to a later time. My normal pace of running around to organize getting ready for the flight was impossible with the shock running through my body.

My housemate, who was home at the time offered to drive me to the airport.

"Thanks, you are a lifesaver."

At the check-in, the attendant informed me, "You have missed your flight that was scheduled for 10am which means you won't be able to fly out for another four hours."

I objected, "My friend said she would change the flight to a later one as I was in shock and unable to get here in time."

"We have no record of this."

After explaining the details of my delay and the reason for my urgency in flying to Melbourne, the steward suggested going upstairs to another check-in section for availability on the next flight. Upstairs once more being informed it was impossible to get an earlier flight, my declaration of the circumstances was again affirmed. The attendant suggested there was not much hope, as the flight was full.

Waiting on a nearby seat, I experienced an overwhelming feeling that there was room for me on that flight. I was very lucky because within ten minutes the attendant booked me on the plane in first class which was a new experience for me.

I thanked my housemate for his help before following the air hostess to the plane; you can probably imagine the surprise in my demeanour, to find an aisle seat with plenty of room for my feet. There was one seat between myself and the lady sitting in the window seat. We nodded to each other as we made eye contact. Sitting down, an air hostess greeted me and suggested a drink. I ordered a red wine. One of my friends had given me a small book to read. She said it would be good to read before arriving in Melbourne. The book was about death and grieving; which affected me emotionally after reading only a few pages, making the continuance unbearable.

For the rest of the journey the tears flowed incessantly. The air hostess kept bringing me handfuls of tissues.

Arriving in Melbourne, after collecting my baggage, the taxi queue was long. Turning around behind me, there was a young couple who instinctively starting chatting and my intention of sharing a cab came to fruition as they were going in the same direction.

We took the next taxi and travelled to the hospital. The young couple had just returned from an overseas holiday very eager to tell me all about it, which was just the distraction desired, to take my mind away from the inevitable confronting me. Arriving at my destination I gave the couple some money for my contribution of the journey and bid them farewell, with a safe trip home.

Finding my father's room at the hospital and walking inside, he was unconscious and breathing heavily. I made it, he was still alive.

Walking over to his bed, I bent to kiss him on the cheek, realizing he was unable to speak. Setting up a chair next to the bed, sitting down and grabbing his hand, noticing the marks on his skin where the drip must have been set into his vein; my reaction was to stroke his forearm.

"Dad, I love you. I finally arrived after a few hiccups and you waited for me. I heard you calling my name early this morning, just before I fell asleep. I knew you would wait for me."

From then on, I was waffling about what was happening in Brisbane. Holding his arm and massaging it gently the whole time my lips were moving.

I said to him, "It's time for you to let go of this life, Dad. Mum will be waiting for you in the spirit world."

My hands kept massaging his arm and repeating similar words, over and over again. Suddenly I was interrupted by the ringing of my mobile phone that was not turned off, which was a hospital rule, but forgotten in all the excitement of attaining my goal.

Answering and acknowledging my brother Ashley, I uttered, "Hold on for a moment as I am sitting with Dad at the hospital."

Leaving the room, looking around the hospital and finding a little alcove through a double door to the outside, gave me a unique area to talk. Ashley was still in Sydney. He didn't want to visit Dad and see him in this condition. He wanted his own memories of when he last saw him at Easter. We spoke for many minutes. Ashley very rarely kept in contact with anyone although there was an instant understanding between the two of us. Maybe that was because we are both Scorpio. He felt more comfortable talking with me about this situation. He rang me three times over the next couple of days.

After speaking with Ashley and returning to my father, the repetition of the same words flowed from my mouth. There was urgency in my voice to make sure when he passed this world, he would go towards the white light to greet our mother who had passed away 24 years previously. He probably thought, "why is she repeating herself?"

This was the appropriate time for me to tell my father what was in store for him when he passed on. When I first received the message from the spirit about his death and the message to give him, my thoughts were to tell him straight away. On the contrary, in the end the communication was explained just before he died. He did die of a heart attack in less than two years, after receiving the message from the spirit.

Sometimes messages need to be left alone and not acted upon as the circumstances will appear when needed. This type of communication about death is not a normal spiritual response. As mentioned before, I believe this message was given because of my prediction, that he wouldn't live to his 80th birthday.

Eventually, after being with my father for some time; noticing the clock situated on the wall, it was 9pm. My brother Josh suggested staying at his flat during my visit to Melbourne and the clock was suggesting it was time to leave. Saying goodbye to Dad with the reassurance of my return tomorrow was difficult, notwithstanding my issue of leaving him; however, knowing he needed to digest all the mumbo jumbo being thrust at him, made it easier to leave.

It was great to see my brothers and sister. A tragedy like this brings families even closer. The family decided to meet early the next morning to visit Dad in hospital. The next morning just as we were about to walk out the door, the phone rang. It was the hospital to say that Dad had just passed away.

The tears are rolling down my face writing this, almost reliving the event.

Josh, Brendan and I huddled together and cried. We knew he was in a better place; however, no matter how much one is prepared, the emotions always take us by surprise.

Eventually we walked out of Josh's flat to be greeted by Maureen and her husband and Amanda, their daughter, enabling all of us to travel in one car to the hospital.

We walked into the hospital room and surrounded the bed, each taking hold of his hand or arm. His mouth was open and his body was still warm.

After a little while, moving around to the other side, around the end of the bed, there was a feeling of coolness in the room. Just above my father's head there was a small circle of warmth; on looking more closely the circle was a yellowish mist thicker than the air, and was a phenomenon to me.

I called out, "His spirit has left his body and that warm patch above his head is his spirit. This body is a dead body, with no soul. Dad's spirit has left his body so there is no need for me to be here anymore. I'll meet you at the café for breakfast."

My family looked at me aghast as though I had just flipped. They met me for breakfast a little while later. We spent that afternoon organizing funeral arrangements and ringing family and friends.

The next day was Thursday. My decision was to walk down the main street towards the shopping centre, where a beauty salon was situated for me to have my eyelashes tinted; instead of using mascara which could run down my face, if the tears flowed during the funeral. After the treatment slowly walking back along the road, towards Josh's house, which was about six blocks, there was an awareness of two people walking behind me. They seemed so close that my automatic response was to look behind on the right side but there was no-one there; immediately looking on my left side and again no-one there.

My mind was confused as I could have sworn footsteps were behind me. Mystified by this experience and definitely confused, when suddenly my father's spirit loomed on my right side and grabbed my hand. Instantaneously my mother's spirit grabbed my left hand. To the reader this sounds unfathomable; nevertheless this was a tangible presence. I could feel their hands in mine, although light like a feather.

My experience was of a little girl again, about three years old, with Mummy and Daddy walking me down the street. This was the most exciting miracle that has ever happened to me.

We talked as one does catching up on chit chat as we journeyed along the road. This was the main road in Sandringham with many cars driving past.

I said to them, "I'm sure the people in those cars think I am crazy, talking to myself."

It was a ten minute walk to my brother's house and we talked the whole time. This was a really beautiful experience, talking to my parents as they held my hands. This event just blew me away.

My belief is that father instigated this meeting, letting me know he had heard all my mumbo jumbo and he was now with mum.

Unless one has experienced a special event like this one, it will be hard to comprehend.

Getting closer to Josh's house, my suggestion was to tell the family about this event, (even though my reservations meant my family would think I was crazy) and we laughed together. They both agreed for me to tell the family. I thanked them both for this special encounter as we said our goodbyes.

Laughter comes to mind when I think about the way my family reacted to this encounter. They looked away from me with their thoughts beaming at me, "Oh God, she's really lost her marbles. We'd better ring the nuthouse to see if they have a vacancy."

Quickly I said, "Anyone for tea?" and exited to the kitchen.

That afternoon Brendan and I went shopping for a CD of Al Jolson who was Dad's favourite singer. We decided to play a couple of his songs at the church gathering. We weren't sure if we would find a CD because Al Jolson was a musician from the 50s and 60s however our luck was in, with only one CD left in the shop. I had a feeling Dad had something to do with that, synchronicity came to mind.

That afternoon the family members listened to the CD, singing along to the words. We couldn't believe our ears. We all remembered those words. Yet all those years ago we used to complain to Dad when he wanted to play his Al Jolson music, after all we had just played a Beatles or Stones album. Visualise this: a crowd of 20 teenagers, friends and family members, listening to The Beatles while having a few drinks at my father's home. Once our album was finished Dad would grab his Al Jolson album and insist on playing his music. We would strenuously object without much success.

It was hilarious to realise that even though we objected to his choice of music all those years ago, we remembered all the words to his favourite music. We couldn't stop laughing, remembering how we hated this music. Visualise again, five siblings in a small flat singing along to Al Jolson. I'm sure Dad's spirit was in the room, smiling.

Friday was the big day. We attended a small chapel in Moorabbin, which was packed with people sitting while many more were standing at the back and outside.

My brother Brendan delivered his eulogy first. He kept stopping as the tears welled up in his eyes. I wanted to go up to him and cuddle him. Of course I couldn't. He finished his speech with no more tears.

My little brother Ashley was next and he told some interesting stories of his memories of Dad.

It was my turn to read the fax received from Sue, our sister in Darwin who is now a member of the Hari Krishna movement. She changed her name as is the custom when she joined in the 70s. She knew Dad had gone to the spirit realm and to her there was no need to go to a funeral. She didn't attend our mother's funeral either as she was overseas at the time.

My speech continued with some cherished stories about Dad and also my visit from Mum and Dad the previous day, because of its relevance.

I said, "Most of you probably won't comprehend what I am about to say but this story is too special."

When looking at my siblings in the front row of the church, they watched mortified. I continued with my little story unconcerned with the outcome. On finishing my story, "This incident proves to me that my father came back to tell me he is with Mum and he is okay."

One of my friends put his thumb up in approval. Sitting down, the rest of the ceremony continued.

The guests were invited to attend the burial and the wake afterwards at a Football Club Social Room. My father was buried in the same plot as my mother 24 years earlier. Only close family came to the burial which was appropriate.

Maureen chose the Social Club for the wake because Dad was always involved with football. He was on the Committee of the local Football Club as we were growing up. The club was sold to a league team and my father transferred his energies to the league from then on.

The team he followed in the league was Richmond. After his team folded he religiously followed Richmond, the Mighty Tigers, and attended every game on a Saturday afternoon with esky in hand and his three daughters in tow. As teenagers, we were eager to attend and watch the game although sometimes we were distracted by the talent at the grounds, if you get my drift. My younger brothers attended when they were old enough. If my father wasn't singing the praises of Richmond, he was singing Al Jolson songs with a beer in his hand so it was very appropriate to have those songs at the church service and the wake at a football club.

I remember going to a grand final game at the MCG in the 60's. Richmond won by a point. It was awesome. It was such a close final and everyone was on edge as either team could have won.

The family was divided as far as football teams were concerned. My father, Sue, myself and Brendan, were the Richmond supporters. Maureen and Josh were the Melbourne supporters. Mum never attended because she wasn't really interested in football, although she did attend the grand finale the year Richmond won and the following year when Melbourne won. A week before both games Mum queued for many hours, until Dad arrived after finishing work, relieving Mum in the queue, to purchase tickets for the whole family.

Richmond had not beaten Melbourne for a long time. It just happened that the two teams were playing the night of his wake. The TV was on at the venue and everyone was sneaking a look during the course of the evening. Guess what? Richmond won. Of course they had to win; after all, it was Dad's wake we were celebrating. Maureen told me four years later that Richmond had not beaten Melbourne since Dad's wake.

While in Melbourne for the week of Dad's passing, I developed a new habit. It was July and very mild for a Melbourne winter which prompted me to switch from white to red wine. The beginning of this change to red wine started on the plane journey to Melbourne and continued for the rest of the week, whether it was out to dinner or visiting friends, the red wine flowed. Red wine is still my favourite to this day.

I don't believe in coincidences and these events that occurred were definitely telling a story. This was the initiation of my dead parents talking to me. Sometimes whilst meditating they appear to watch over me or give me a message. They seem to only appear together if there is an important message for me. It's a magical experience and I treasure these contacts.

Through this time of sadness with the tears of a river, time is what heals through the positive memories, to finally acceptance as the cascade trickles along.

Single Parent

The river was fraught with many obstacles constantly twisting and turning, recognizing there was a wider easier flow ahead.

During my life as a single parent, I struggled to make ends meet. Survival seemed to be my motto, although the future envisaged was more opulent. A few of my friends suggested applying for a government subsidized home, although my answer was always the same.

"I know I am extremely strapped for cash most of the time but my thoughts are to purchase my own home someday. I have no idea how this will happen, but I will have my own house one day. Call it intuition."

A few years later I opened a special account with $20 to save for my house. There was never any other amount added to this account. The bills kept rolling in and were paid first, leaving whatever was left to buy food. Sometimes the food wasn't my preference, although it was as healthy as my pocket could afford. Whenever socialising, which was normally dancing, water was mostly consumed with one alcoholic drink unless a kind sir shouted me, which did happen occasionally. My positive attitude kept me steadfast on my journey, knowing that one day success and wealth would prevail.

During this time my neighbour and I became great friends. My compassion for this placid man who had no family to care for him after his wife died, created abundance for me. We became great friends, helping each other as needed over the next ten years, with me eventually caring for him as he became frail with age. He developed a friendship with my children almost akin to a Grandfather. Having never experienced his own children he was delighted to be accompanying them on social occasions. My children wondered why he was with me many times. My answer to this was, "I felt compassion to this gentleman. Besides he needed a good friend, who just happened to be me. I still lead my own life socialising with my friends although there was always time for him."

My help and kindness towards my neighbour initiated a very good friendship and unbeknown to me a house, or was it karma? I believe in karma.

The constant flow of life as with the river concedes knowledge without question.

Pain in My Arm

The waterfall was moving at a rapid pace and falling to the depths in a crash. Once entering the deepness of waters, peace reigned.

During the month of April 2003 my left arm gave me great discomfort, which progressively worsened in the following months. It got so bad that my only solution was to stop working, as massaging clients was aggravating the arm.

Attempting to solve the problem, I decided to book in with my kinesiologist for treatments and massage, but the pain persisted. Eventually she recommended that I see a Feldenkrais therapist, for further treatment on my arm.

In June, speaking with the Feldenkrais therapist on the phone, she advised me on the benefits of this treatment. Convinced this would benefit me, I booked in for a Feldenkrais course that teaches gentle movements to help with injuries. Included in the course was one personal healing treatment, which also grabbed my interest as a secondary solution to my problem.

The course consisted of weekly classes with other participants. When the course was finished, we discussed a date and time for my personal healing which we agreed to be in two weeks' time. Arriving for the appointment, I was taken into a consulting room and advised to lie down on the massage table. She suggested concentrating on my breathing with the intention of gently relaxing the mind. Being familiar with breathing techniques, it didn't take long to feel completely relaxed. During this treatment, an angel appeared and spoke to me.

"You will not return to your employment at The Day Spa."

She then disappeared leaving me wondering what my new position would be.

After my healing was completed, the therapist declared, "While I was healing you, I saw David & Goliath. Does that have any significance to you?"

I said, "I don't know, but maybe David is telling me I need faith and strength for my arm to repair."

Days later when writing, I had an epiphany, with the realization that the reference to David & Goliath, was about writing my book. Thinking about certain events brought up distressing past memories and experiences in my life, which I found hard to bear. For example, going back in my mind 30 years to when my mother died felt strange and eerie, the memory causing me to stop writing, due to the tears overflowing in my eyes. On one such occasion whilst writing about an incident in Canada, this triggered my emotions and before too long the tears were rolling down my face.

Putting down the pen and closing the book led me to go outside, down my stairwell, to the rain forest in the backyard. Walking down the pathway with the stiff dry leaves crunching under my feet, I found myself confronted by the tall smooth trunk of a broad tree. Wrapping my arms around the trunk with my fingers nearly touching, my immediate experience was the tree's energy recharging my batteries. My encounter was so exhilarating that it revitalized energy within my body, comparable to renewed blood running through my veins. My new vigour allowed me to step back inside and continue writing although my decision was to explore a different angle.

This time my emphasis was on the great experiences that occurred in Canada. Once those happy events were down on paper, it was easier to write about the painful times and to see them as disguised lessons.

***

A few days after my healing, my left arm was still causing me great pain. My decision was to rest the arm with the eventual acknowledgement to stop work, at this time. The angel's message was spot-on as I did not return to the day spa after the healing.

Weeks later unable to attend my regular gym routine because of the pain, the footpath became the place of my new morning exercise regime because no matter which direction my arm was moved it caused great angst.

Not long afterwards during a coffee catch up with my Kinesiologist, I mentioned my continuous difficulty. She grabbed my other arm with the intention of muscle testing, to determine which treatment would best suit my condition. The answer she received was a Kinesiology appointment in conjunction with Bach flower remedies. Her suggestion was to make a Bach flower appointment first, then the kinesiology and booked me in for an appointment with her, in two weeks' time.

My naturopath had treated me with Bach flower remedies on other occasions successfully improving the condition. I rang the Naturopathic clinic later that day and managed to book an appointment in the next few days.

A few days later, sitting in the consulting room my naturopath gave me a pack of cards with the written names of Bach flowers on one side and a positive and negative explanation representative of the flower, on the other side. I shuffled the cards and picked out four flowers with one being very significant.

It was "The Star of Bethlehem", and it read:

You have been the victim of extreme shock and the trauma has not left your body.

On the reverse side of the card it read:

I allow my body and soul to rebalance and merge to allow its energy to flow freely.

The tears started to flow while reading the card. The other three cards had no definitive effect on me, but this one was spot on.

She suggested lying on the table and placed a blanket over my body for a 15 to 20 minute healing. I sobbed throughout the whole process, wondering if the tears were ever going to stop.

After the treatment, a little bottle of drops from the Bach flowers chosen was handed to me for consumption during the next few days. Driving home, a slow continuous flow of tears trickled down my face with no end in sight. Arriving home my daughter was confronted with a red eyed monster with tears running down its face with absolutely no way of hiding it. She grabbed me, wrapping her arms around my shoulders with a huge cuddle as I endeavoured to explain my situation. Even her attempt at telling jokes didn't stop my tears. As the week progressed, my tears subsided.

Feeling more in control, my decision was to book a massage before the next kinesiology appointment, hoping to relieve some of the pain. A couple of days later my body was looking forward to the massage. On arrival, I was handed a glass of water and entered the treatment room to allow my preparation before lying on the massage table with a towel for coverage.

During the massage I started to feel quite relaxed with my mind calm, when suddenly the memory of a past life appeared.

Nonchalantly I said, "In a past life session about 14 years ago, I remember going back in time to a life where my arm was chopped off. There is a connection with now and that past life. Maybe I need to forgive the man who chopped off my arm?

"Lynne!" she yelled with recognition in her voice. We both knew there was a connection with this past life. She continued with the massage in silence giving both of us time to think about the prospect of the next appointment.

Finally, on the 11th September driving to my kinesiology appointment my thoughts were…this appointment won't take very long because of visiting this lifetime before. Gee was I wrong!

Parking the car on the opposite side of the road to the premises, my mind was still of the opinion that this wouldn't take long. I walked across the road and knocked on the door. The door was opened with a welcoming smile, directing me towards the consulting room.

With this appointment one does not need to disrobe. Lying on the massage table, my body was muscle tested to make sure it was balanced, before continuing with the treatment.

"Think about the pain in your arm," said the kinesiologist.

Concentrating on the pain, my mind returned immediately to the relevant past life.

"In this past life, I am a child in ancient Japan and only eight years old. My left arm has been chopped off at the shoulder and because of the great loss of blood, I died instantly. My body is lying on the ground as my spirit leaves the body. Being in spirit form enables me to look down on the situation (once we die, our spirit leaves the body and watches from above)."

The following events I am now witnessing occur after my death with my spirit's direction (I have the ability to hear my spirit talking).

"My master is sorry. He didn't mean to kill me; he just wanted to stop me running away. Looking at my master, I realise that he was treated badly as a child and does not know any better. I forgive him for cutting off my arm and after a short moment forgive him for being a harsh master. The latter is the hardest to forgive."

Within seconds of leaving the past life I become very upset and can't stop crying, although eventually compose myself and utter to my kinesiologist, "I am upset because my mother will not know about my death."

"Return to the past life and see what transpires." said the kinesiologist.

I focus on the past life again. "I can see my mother returning to the fence. She knows something is wrong. She looks at my body lying on the ground but is not allowed to enter. She is dragged away screaming. My body is picked up to be carted away."

"Is your arm with you?" asked my kinesiologist.

"No, it's on the ground."

"Pick up your arm," the kinesiologist uttered with concern in her voice.

"I visualise myself picking up the arm and putting it on my person. After this incident, my master is a changed man.

Ostracized from the village, my mother is not allowed to go to my funeral although three days later my master allows her to see where I am buried. She visits the grave every day and eventually my master permits her to return to the village. Subsequently she meets a man and marries again. She has a daughter named Ishi. At that moment, I know that I am in Japan, in the year 1652 and my mother lives in the town of Haasa. My mother is happy again as she visits my grave with her new daughter every day.

I am happy knowing my mother returned to witness the aftermath of my death and my master has allowed her to live in the community again. She is now living a new life and my master is a kinder man. Consequently, my death is not in vain."

"Do you need to revisit this life again?" asked the kinesiologist.

"No, I don't think so."

"I am ending the session now because I think you have conquered enough today."

Within a few days my arm felt much better and after that kinesiology session the problems with my arm disappeared. It was like magic.

This incident was a very powerful experience and one I had not undergone before. The pain in my arm triggered a past life event mentioned in the chapter on Counselling – Past Life experiences. My past life memories took some time to surface although once I had revisited and rectified the event, by visually picking up the arm off the ground and attaching it to the shoulder, I found I had a pain free arm within days.

We may not utilize all of our brain, however my belief is; locked away in part of the brain are our past memories of lives that can unravel mysteries in this life.

The peacefulness after the storm was welcome as life continued in a comfortable flow.

Meditation Messages

Time spent in the tranquil waters allows the body and brain to go within and enjoy serenity.

During the month of July, I attended my regular meditation class which was held on a Wednesday.

The facilitator had the ability to take us on a visual journey. Once relaxed he suggested, "Visualise a field with a large tree. Branching off from the tree visualise a door. Open the door and walk into the room, where you will find some clothing on a chair. Change into the clothing."

Looking at my chair there was a cape draped over it with a crown on the seat. Picking up the cape I covered my shoulders and placed the crown on my head.

Our instruction was, "Climb down the stairs that are ahead."

In my case the stairs were actually going up so I ascended the stairs.

"At the bottom of the stairs there is another door which leads to a room. Open the door and take note of the type of door. What is behind the door?" asked the facilitator.

My door was round and led into a spaceship. Sitting down on a huge chair, the realization set in that I was the King. The advice given to me was that I had an abundance of knowledge to pass onto the Kingdom. This knowledge which was within my mind, enabled me to create anything I wished for and held me in great esteem by the people. I was almost worshipped. The power was for good.

Just after receiving this message the facilitator spoke.

"Come out of the room, making your way up the stairs and back to the field. Take your time to come back to your chair in this room." The meditation finished and we discussed our various journeys.

My feelings are that this meditation, referred to my knowledge which influenced me to write this book.

* * *

During the month of August, Brisbane holds a huge fair, named Ekka (a shortening of the word exhibition) which lasts for ten days annually. Country folk bring their cattle and stock into the city for the big competition.

Rides, food, competition, animals, exhibits and fashion parades are some of the events. Show bags are a big part of this event. Many businesses use this marketing tool to sell their products. A majority of the show bags are full of lollies and of course the children love them.

Wednesday morning was my meditation class; however, being Ekka holiday most of the group wanted to have the day off. The facilitator said he would still take the group if anyone was interested.

On the day, there was just myself and one other participant. The facilitator decided to give one of us a healing. I was chosen and the other participant helped with the healing. My intent was to balance my spirit. I lay on the table with blankets over my body to keep warm.

"Think about your intent."

While relaxing and thinking about my intent, a fly flew into the room. This fly kept flying around my face. My hand kept shooing it away, but it wouldn't go. I stopped shooing the fly and asked, "What do you want to tell me?"

I thought it wanted me to fly away so I started to visualize flying in the sky. But the fly kept buzzing around me so I asked again, "What are you trying to tell me?"

The fly landed on my face and the word that came to me was: LISTEN. I listened intently and straight away I could hear a bird singing with a beautiful shrill sound.

I then heard a spirit speak. "You must write your book for at least two hours a day and it must be finished by December." I was mystified. This message was repeated to me several times.

"It is very important for people to know what you have to say. You used to write Hebrew Scriptures in a past life."

Feeling deeply relaxed when the healing was finished, made it difficult to feel present in the room. It seemed many minutes passed before I was able to open my eyes.

This meditation was encouraging me to keep writing as the knowledge and experience to write had already been obtained in a past life. At that time the book was in its infancy and my writing was in longhand.

* * *

It was nearing the end of August and I had another meditation class. My thoughts were, "I have no plans after this class, which will enable me to spend a lot of time writing." Somehow that didn't happen.

This class was special because our facilitator invited a musician. The musician, who was heavily bearded, tall and lanky, except for his podge in the belly, had a very amiable smile. He was going to play music while we meditated. He was quite a contrast to our facilitator, who was about 172 cms and very robust and round. He was barefoot today and wore a colourful sari, which seemed to be his uniform on each of my attendance. His head was currently shaved, making this one of his many facades.

Our group consisted of six people. We sat in a circle on chairs with cushions. The facilitator started the meditation by asking us to close our eyes, straighten our backs and take a few deep breaths in and out to relax the body. The angels were brought in for protection along with the white light and our guides. He set our intention of clearing past or present blocks.

During the meditation, my first visualisation was of myself in Egypt as a dancer with flowing robes. That must be why I love to dance in this present life.

The musician was walking around each person playing different instruments. My body started shaking and twitching as he approached me, suddenly taking my mind back in time to a past life in ancient Egypt.

There were two chariots racing in a circled pavilion. I was a three-year-old child amongst the crowd, watching the race with my mother. I witnessed the two chariots crashing into each other, causing the death of the two men. One of those men was my father. A few days later there was a procession for the burial.

While sitting in my chair in the present life, I suddenly became increasingly stressed as he played his music around me. With tears descending down my face, my body was shaking and turned a complete 90 degree angle, facing the back of my chair. My hands covered my face, aware that I was disturbing the other members of the meditation group, except unable to move out of this space. Minutes later, I calmed down and turned around to the front again as my body started rocking.

During my experience of this past life, I was in my mother's arms, resisting her command to look at the procession of the funeral. Friends of my mother were coaching me to look around; however, I kept hiding my face. Eventually, whilst giving me a huge cuddle my mother said, "Now I am going to look after you."

That cuddle started to release the anguished feelings. There were whispers that people were pleased my father was dead. They believed my mother had married below her station and weren't happy about the marriage.

The anguish I was feeling was connected to the child's situation in the past life. Soon afterwards the facilitator suggested, "Wiggle your toes and hands, gently bringing your energy back into the room."

All the participants in the room felt my anguish and wanted to help, although they knew it was not acceptable to touch me while in a meditative state.

Through tears I sniffled to the group, "I apologize for disturbing your meditation."

They were very concerned for me. The facilitator suggested, "Lynne, do you wish to talk about your experience now or later?"

"Later please."

The tears kept flowing down my face and my body was still shaking as the class continued. When it was my turn to relay my journey, the tears still flowed down my face, with an eerie feeling that there was more to this story.

Once each person relayed their experience, the facilitator asked the musician if he had felt anything whilst moving around each person.

"I play the musical instruments to suit the energy encompassed in the group. I did not feel anything else while walking around playing my instruments."

While he was talking, our eyes met and we were in a trance with neither able to look away. My eyes were fixated and could not move.

The facilitator asked him, "Can you see a spirit?"

He didn't say anything and everyone looked in my direction as I quickly looked away. The musician made a quick exit as soon as the meditation class finished. I felt he was involved somehow in my past life – maybe the other chariot rider!

The facilitator suggested, "Lynne, you should verbally forgive yourself and the other people involved in that past life, sometime within the next few days."

Driving home took me about 20 minutes with my thoughts pondering the understanding of the past life just visited. Arriving home with my thoughts still transfixed, there was only one decision to make.

Sitting on the chair, relaxing with gentle breathing techniques enabled a calmness to transcend throughout my physique.

With this quiet tranquillity, empowerment facilitated an easy transition to the past life, where forgiveness was needed for the participants and me to heal. My intuition felt strongly that my father was murdered by the other chariot rider, except it backfired with both being killed.

This was my first time of travelling back into a past life while meditating. The facilitator said I have a gift, being able to materialise past lives.

I have meditated to varying degrees since my initial instruction at age thirty. In the beginning relaxing the mind was a very complexing encounter. With repetition, wondrous releases of the voices in the brain can actually happen. Allowing this release enables me to sometimes receive messages from spirits, advising me of future events, although not given a time frame. Receiving these messages instigated thoughts of immediate correlation; on the contrary, most of them are dealing with long term future.

* * *

The following messages which I have received through meditation are yet to materialise.

One occasion was Friday 14th October 2005 with a group of three friends attending an arranged meetup with the intention of meditating. The four of us arranged our chairs in a circle and began to breathe deeply to relax our bodies, with our eyes closed. Our facilitator suggested a peaceful surrounding with the following being my experience.

During our relaxed state a male spirit spoke to me.

"This is the house for you to buy." My vision was of a beautiful house.

"Where is this house?" I asked.

"Indooroopilly," he said.

"I thought I could only afford a flat."

"The house is two-storey with trees in the backyard and a window on the top level looking out towards the Brisbane River. You will work on one floor and live on the other."

Nowadays upon receiving messages, my automatic response is to jot the details into a book for future reference, as it may take years for the event to occur.

* * *

Exactly a week later on the 20th October, I sat down at home to meditate. It took me a while to relax and go into a meditative state as the room felt dishevelled, whereupon my first thought was to ask all the spirits in the room, without good intentions for my soul, to leave. The energy soon changed in the room especially with the help of breathing out the stale energy and breathing in the new life energy. Concentrating on this process, a beautiful spirit floated into the room and spoke to me.

She said, "The house you will buy is exactly how you imagine. You will love it. You need to rest for these things to happen and you need to believe. Gather strength. You will be in this house for a long time and there will be another. You will have freedom to write, teach and love. You must write information down." She then floated out of the room as she had originally entered.

Gradually, I moved my fingers and toes, then eventually the rest of my body, before opening my eyes, to a feeling of exhilaration and joy, at this wonderful prospect, but when?

* * *

One month later during another meditation at home, a spirit who called herself Sheila spoke.

She said, "You will be moving into your house in February. It will be the first house you look at and you'll know it's the one. Don't rush yourself. You need time out to heal. Start to organise yourself."

I thought, "Wow! February, that doesn't give me much time." February came and went with me wondering which year she meant.

That was the third time this similar message was given to me. Whenever messages are given to me three times they will definitely occur. That means this house is coming sometime in the future.

* * *

A few years later I started attending a new meditation group.

I arrived at 7pm even though the class did not start until 7.30pm, gee was that eagerness?

A CD by Deepak Chopra was playing. It was very loud which grated on my ears at first, nevertheless, I slowly mellowed to the sound. Five minutes later the volume was turned down to facilitate a guided meditation with instruction to go beyond the universe high in the sky. My vision was of myself as Queen of Sheba dressed in pink feathers. The meditation went for one hour. Fifteen minutes before we finished, my body was fidgety and wondering when it was going to finish.

Concentrating on relaxing deeper into the meditation, within a short time, a spirit spoke to me. "You will be healing and teaching the young. These children and young adults will be in their teens and twenties. Your healing abilities will take you around the world. You will live in a two-storey house in Indooroopilly, with views of the river; working on the bottom floor and living above. The work area will be luxurious, as is the top floor." As the spirit spoke these words I found myself actually in the house, looking out towards the river. It was just like watching a movie except my presence was in it.

Shortly afterwards the facilitator guided us back to the room. This was definitely a reassurance that something bigger and better was to come. My life has changed radically in the last six months since clearing my energy to allow love and success into my life. This was a very empowering meditation.

The tranquil waters gave me insight into my life and the future to come.

Career Change

Sometimes life throws us an opportunity and we have no idea why or how it can be achieved. The waters are running quite smoothly; then suddenly there is a change in direction as a boat rushes by, causing the waves in the river to rise and fall.

It was August 2006 and I was sharing with a girl-friend who owned the house. To me this time of year heralded the end of winter, as the warmer days took over. I walked outside to the huge balcony which over-looked the tree-lined back yard, again appreciating my luck of living in these beautiful, peaceful surrounds in a double storey house, sharing with a friend. Sitting down on one of the large comfortable outdoor chairs, I had made the decision to relax and meditate as no-one else was home. As my body calmed through the breathing technique, I very quickly melted into a serene meditative state. Shortly into the meditation a voice spoke to me:

"Go and give readings. Go and give readings. Go and give readings."

My voice box didn't utter a word. These words were not expected as I slowly brought my mind back to my earthly surrounds. Opening my eyes, my thoughts were…those statements must be important because they were repeated three times. Being psychic, I quite often give messages to my friends or clients, except giving readings is a whole new career path. I have the ability to heal with my hands especially if someone has a headache or pain from an injury. My thoughts were; maybe giving readings is another important healing method.

Thinking about this message, my memory bank went back to a crystal shop frequented with friends at my local shopping centre, where readers were employed.

"Maybe they need readers. That was a place to start."

The next day I drove to Indooroopilly and parked in the shopping centre car park. The shop was on the third floor, not far from my parking spot. Walking to the shop and stopping outside; peering through the window to perceive any activity and noticing only one person in the shop, I ventured in. Strutting up to the counter my courage took over, allowing me to ask the manager, "Do you need any psychic readers at the moment?"

She said, "Not at the moment; although Jane may not be coming in on Saturday because she has been ill. Give me your phone number. I'll call you for a trial if she is unavailable."

I jotted down my name and phone number on the piece of paper she handed me.

I said, "thank you" as my shaky legs walked out of the shop, albeit feeling good at accomplishing this task. A couple of days later the lady from the shop rang.

"Can you give readings on Saturday for part of the day?"

My response was, "Yes".

Arriving just before 9am, she had bookings for most of Saturday and my experience was very enjoyable. After that day, there were no more phone calls from the shop and my resolve was that the spirit's message was referring to that one day.

In the meantime, an acquaintance gave me a business card of a psychic working in Brisbane. One day when shopping, I dropped into the shop to investigate. Walking over to the manager and introducing myself, we chatted for some time. Before leaving she asked for my phone number to be written at the back of her book. My reaction was quite bizarre; mentioning my wish to work as a reader.

About two months later whilst meditating, again the same message:

"Go and give readings. Go and give readings. Go and give readings."

I was astonished. Why do I need to give readings? The next morning after having slept on these statements my decision was to visit the manager of the shop I had visited recently.

Feeling very nervous entering the shop, my face lit up as she recognised me. The manager immediately said, "Hello Jenny, I've been trying to contact you but I couldn't find your number."

"My name is Lynne; that's probably why you couldn't find me. I wrote my name and number in the back of the book."

"Never mind, you're here now. I would like you to work on Sunday and Monday, giving readings."

My new career commenced the following Sunday and somehow subconsciously, this shop was my new direction in life although there was a need for a prompt from my spirits.

My commitment in the shop was for nine months before venturing to another group of psychics who travelled around to many shopping centres. This experience enabled me to travel around Brisbane and the Gold Coast for a period of nearly three years. I now give readings and healings from my home.

About 12 years ago, a girlfriend invited me to dinner at her home. After our delicious meal and sipping on champagne she decided to go outside for a cigarette. I stayed inside sitting on a chair with the security door separating us, chatting about her house hunting. Then suddenly I blurted out this information:

"The next house you see will be yours. It's in a suburb starting with the letter M. Once you move in and make plans for renovations, your partner will ask you to marry him. You will be married within the next two years and will have a baby boy."

We both looked at each other questioningly, as she didn't want children. "I have channelled this information for you unknowingly, so the angels knew you needed to hear this. Just wait and see what happens."

Within three months they were moving into their new abode just around the corner from where they lived in Mt. Gravatt. I was invited to the wedding and asked to be the makeup artist for the bridesmaids. She did have a baby boy, except it was a dog.

Another good friend who is a Feng Shui consultant visited me one day to give me some decorating suggestions for my apartment. Just before leaving she asked to book a reading.

A couple of weeks later during her reading I said, "There is a plant near the front of your garden that isn't very healthy. It needs to be moved to another area where there is more sunlight. Your instinct will tell you where to put it."

She said, "I think I know the plant you mean and it has been struggling although there isn't any need to move it. I need to look after it more."

I had never visited this house before. "I'll leave it with you although there is an urgency to move it."

A few months later we caught up and she said, "I eventually did as you suggested and moved that plant to the rear side of the house. It is thriving now as it is getting more sun. Thank you."

To me giving readings is helping individuals with difficulties that arise in the now and near future. If there are decisions on which way to go, my guidelines are suggested to help that person in their decision making.

The information I receive is channelled from the client's angels. This knowledge is what the client needs to hear and sometimes my medium abilities transmit messages from a departed relative or friend. I am the vehicle to pass on the communication.

Since giving more intuitive readings I have incorporated my healing abilities to some treatments. As my abilities develop, the experiences become more attuned to the higher beings of the universe.

My sister Maureen lost her son six months before she visited me. During her break for a week, I suggested giving her a healing. My thoughts were that the spirit of her son would appear. She accepted my invitation. Very soon after starting the healing her son was by my side and I relayed his messages to her.

He said, "Mum, just before I died I yelled out your name."

I could feel the tears growing in my eyes as he continued speaking. It was a very moving experience for me because of my relationship with her and my nephew.

He then uttered, "When you return and move into your new home, I will be waiting in the morning at your back veranda, as you sip your tea before driving to work."

Once the healing was finished she said, "How did he know that I had a new home? I have only just purchased it."

It is amazing, although once in the spirit world, they see and hear everything.

A day later she said to me "I would never have thought that I needed a healing. I am so glad you suggested it. I'm feeling so much more accepting of his death and coping seems easier. Thank you so much."

I was invited to visit a client from my meditation group for a few days in the country. This seemed like a great getaway from the buzz of the city. After travelling in torrential rain it was pleasing to see a dryer sky on arrival at the two-storey cottage, where both of us wanted some peace and relaxation.

During my sojourn, meditation was on the agenda. This particular meditation on the day before leaving was quite remarkable. I proceeded through the relaxation technique of slowing down the nervous system, enabling the body and mind to switch off from normal activity, taking us to our meditative state. Then suddenly there in front of me was a vision of Archangel Gabriel. He was standing in front of me with real feathers adorned over his huge wings.

"I am here to help you in any way I can."

"Thank you," I said, with my vision fixated on those huge wings. I was staring at this magnificent angel feeling so privileged and in awe of his beauty. From memory, he stood on the left-hand side of God with Archangel Michael on the right. Wow, what an apparition.

A few days later back in the city, progressing through my emails, I noticed one from Doreen Virtue and it just happened to be about Archangel Gabriel. I downloaded the free article which demonstrated his healing abilities, one of which was conception. To my astonishment, I found a chapter on his capabilities connected with writers. I believe this is why he appeared.

Whilst meditating alone one morning I asked Archangel Gabriel to help me in my quest to publish my book. A few weeks later a friend of mine suggested attending a writers group, which met once a month. During my visits to this group I found the information very insightful, initiating the decision to divide my book into two. My thanks to Archangel Gabriel were spoken with exhilarated gratitude.

The next week meditating with my client, I experienced the vision of not only Archangel Gabriel but also Archangel Michael, letting me know that they are around to help whenever needed. The message was to ask and you shall receive.

I find whenever I ask angels to find me a car park there is always a park in the street or in front of the building I am attending. As long as I am grateful, the angels will help in any way they can.

Half an hour before Jan arrived for a healing I walked into my healing room and cleared any negative energy.

Sitting in my chair I proceeded to welcome any spirits or guides connected to Jan. Looking around the room there was a man (spirit) who was her father. Instinctively I knew he wanted to speak to her. Twenty minutes later, Jan arrived for her appointment. During Jan's healing her father spoke.

"I haven't got long for this world," he said.

I felt that he was preparing her for the inevitable.

Jan said, "I felt his time was coming up, after all, he is 88. I wanted to book a flight to see him maybe at Christmas."

"I think it would be wise to book straight away and phone him with the news. He will be very pleased."

Jan said, "I will go to the travel agent tomorrow and book. Thank you so much for that message."

More than 10 years ago, whilst meditating, I was able to speak to a male spirit on many occasions even though he was still living on earth. This message from Jan's father was the first time during a healing session that the spirit was still alive here on earth.

The next day I faced a similar occurrence. My client originally booked for a lesson on meditation and then the day before, she rang to see if the appointment could be changed to a healing session as a few things had occurred since her last healing. As Mondays are not busy, there was plenty of time to accommodate her request.

During the healing a man's spirit stood next to me. He was from her past and appeared in her healing, as he wished to be forgiven for a situation that occurred many years ago. He also mentioned that he would like to visit her in the next few years. This was very emotional for her although she was forgiving. I believe this was the reason she needed a healing to enable him to surface and discuss past issues. In the last healing, this event impacted on her heart being broken. The healing released the energy connected to this incident therefore releasing the broken heart empowering her to move on with life.

These stories are just a few of the phenomena I experience from my clients, who have agreed to be in this book.

The river eventually accepted the rush of water as it released the waves and subsided back to its normal flow.

I am the Messenger

Life is full of surprises as is the river changing and twisting with new experiences to tantalise.

It was January 2008 and my mind was preoccupied with work situations. My thoughts were interrupted by the phone ringing. It was a phone call from Melbourne informing me that a close friend of mine, Andy had been killed in a motorbike accident.

Andy and I celebrated the same birthday on 26th October, although Andy was a year younger than me. My ex-husband and I met Andy and his wife whilst living in the same block of flats in Melbourne, many years ago. Both our spouses were Aquarian although not celebrated on the same day. Over the years, Andy or I would spontaneously ring, sometimes before or after the actual birth date even after both our marriages had ended. It was an unwritten custom between two friends.

The last birthday we spoke was in 2007. Andy rang with the birthday wishes and during our conversation he informed me of his rare cancer which instigated his second marriage to Maria in a small ceremony. There was elation, of course, to hear about the marriage, but hidden shock by his description of the cancer. As he spoke of his cancer my heart felt crushed, acknowledging to myself that he wouldn't be living much longer. I rang him several weeks later, just before Christmas, to see how he was. He was always a very humorous person and had me in stitches, not really wanting me to know how much pain he was in. A few weeks later, he was dead.

My wish was to be part of the ceremony celebrating Andy's life. The discovery over years of meditating was that one could obtain a resolution when one's mind was at peace. Sauntering outside to the deck, my favourite chair for meditating was waiting. Sitting down it was easy to relax into a deep meditation. Suddenly, I saw a figure in front of me and recognized the spirit of Andy.

He said, "Lynne, I've been trying to talk to Maria, but she's not listening. I can't seem to communicate with her. She needs to know that I didn't purposely kill myself because of the cancer. It was a motorbike accident. She doesn't seem to understand me. Can you explain and convince her?"

"Yes, of course I can. I'll talk to her during my visit to Melbourne for your funeral." That truly was a bizarre statement. With that, he disappeared.

I slowly brought myself back into the room by moving slightly and sensing my feet and hands, then the rest of my body. Once feeling comfortable back in my chair, my eyes opened. I felt quite elated and surprised that Andy's spirit contacted me, knowing my decision to go to Melbourne was absolute.

After booking the flight; arrangements were made with my brother, Brendan, to stay for a couple of days. The funeral was on the day after I arrived, which started with a long train ride towards the Dandenong Mountains near Olinda. On my arrival at the ceremony, new faces surrounded me with a few familiar ones as well. There was a huge screen on the wall above the altar showing Andy's life.

Later at the wake which was conveniently across the road, I approached a family member offering my condolences. During our conversation, the message for Maria was mentioned although he was most adamant for me to wait a few days before confronting her. This sounded feasible, although I didn't have a few days.

Sometime later when Maria approached me; this was the opportunity to tell her and perceive her reaction. Putting my arms around her to console her, we hugged for a few seconds before getting straight to the point of me being there.

"I have a message for you from Andy. He spoke to me whilst meditating a couple of days ago."

Maria suggested meeting in half an hour after some of the guests had left. Maria appeared half an hour later, as I excused myself from the discussion with other guests. She grabbed my arm and led me to an outside room where we could be alone and talk. We hugged each other again.

I declared, "After being informed of the news about Andy I decided to meditate and as soon as my body was deeply relaxed, Andy's spirit appeared in front of me. He was concerned that you would think he had committed suicide because of his cancer. Andy was most adamant that you know it was an accident. He was trying desperately to connect with you, which is the reason he spoke to me. I have a gift of hearing the departed souls."

Maria was overwhelmed, "I could see this beautiful white light in our bedroom, surrounding the bed. The bedroom was lit up like a Christmas tree. I knew it was Andy, although I didn't realise he was talking to me. I thought he was letting me know he was alright. Thank you so much, Lynne. It is such a relief to know it was an accident. I never thought he would take his own life. He was such a positive person, always thinking of others. He was in a lot of pain and his stomach was expanding, because of the cancer. He probably misjudged the road causing the accident."

Maria asked me to contact her again if any more messages materialised, although there have been no more. Andy needed Maria to know the truth about what happened and I was the conduit. This experience was an honour, empowering me to perform a duty of messenger.

Once the revelations of the situation are acknowledged the river of life is then in harmony.

Blood Pressure

The river has a certain direction in which it flows, the same as the blood throughout our body and when it is disturbed the highs and lows can appear.

I have found on many occasions during this life, my blood pressure has risen quite high. These times seem to coincide with stressful events. My blood pressure was high a few weeks before giving birth to my two children. I fell in my backyard in 2005; causing extremely high blood pressure, precipitating a few years on medication. It didn't sit well with me to be on medication so my journey was to search for other alternatives.

Over the years, I have used several alternative methods for my blood pressure along with diet, exercise and meditation. I feel these have contributed to my healthier life. Because of the alternative methods my blood pressure lowered and I now continue to use them, along with my affirmation:- "I am healthy, wealthy and wise". Whatever we feed our mind it will accept, so there is no other alternative but to give it positive words. This alternative way is my way of dealing with my health and may not be suitable for everyone.

This is what culminated during a counselling session. At the beginning of this session the therapist determined that the emotion "threatened" was the issue for this treatment.

Through deep breathing my mind immediately journeyed back, revisiting a past life where I was involved in a train wreck with no significant injuries; except my concussed state of mind from a bang on the head. Intuitively knowing the other survivors and I should move forward from the wreck, I was unable to convince them because of my condition.

The survivors of the train crash were uneasy about my advice especially the three young boys who suggested going back to the start of our journey. With the help of a female survivor who convinced them to take my advice, we eventually arrived at our destination. My companions were pleased to have accepted the instruction, once learning we were the only survivors.

The session closed (this event was similar to my fall in 2005, also being concussed with the blood pressure rising quite dangerously). It took more than 2 years for me to recover completely.

* * *

It was September, the beginning of spring with beautiful blue skies and the start of longer sunny days. Whilst on the phone in communication with my counsellor/therapist she suggested another session to sort out my blood pressure issue.

Today was my appointment and I was convinced the underlying reason for my blood pressure would surface. Arriving early, my therapist was on the phone sorting out an appointment which enabled me to grab a cup of tea and enjoy some me time. Finishing the phone call, we both walked to the treatment room and sat down to discuss my aims for today.

"I am rather upset over the death of Brian."

Brian, my neighbour was like a father figure, especially since my father passed in 1999. I was his friend and carer and he thought of me as the substitute daughter he never had. It was only six weeks since he had passed and it was me who found his body.

Lying on the table, we proceeded with the session as the word "freedom" came into my mind.

My mind took me back to my ten-year-old self swinging on a huge tree in the backyard of the family home. My mother urged me to climb down because she thought it was dangerous. My enjoyment was being stopped on every occasion that I attempted a new encounter and the result was losing my freedom. This was my experience to swing on the tree, with the outcome being my lesson.

"Visualize you on the swing having fun," said the therapist.

I was really happy to be free, flying in the air, with no injuries as I visualised being on a swing. It was so much fun and even today, if I get a chance I will swing in the park bringing back memories of being a child.

In another event, my parents would not allow me to visit a school friend because she lived on a main road. A little white lie was told to my parents. I said I was visiting a girlfriend in the next street. Instead of going to visit her, I walked to my friend's house on the main road. Walking towards her house, a huge dog ran towards me and I froze with fright. This is not the way to react with a big dog. He felt my fear and bit me. I ran to my friend's house and her mother put an antiseptic lotion on my bite. The day was so much fun, however big trouble greeted me on arriving home. My parents visited the other family only to discover I wasn't there. They argued that I was the eldest and should set an example to the younger children.

I was asked to relive the event the way I would have preferred. My visualization of the event was being driven by my father to my friend's house, enabling me to be safe from the busy road without any confrontation with the dog.

For my sixteenth birthday party my parents allowed me to invite some friends from school. I also invited a girl who was new to the school and didn't have many friends. My other friends thought I was stupid inviting the boring girl.

I said, "She doesn't have many friends because she is new to the school and I feel sorry for her." The poor girl obviously felt the energies from the other girls and left early.

One of the girls, who was very tall and brought her boyfriend, thought she was very clever. Unbeknown to her, the boyfriend asked me to go for a walk and gave me a kiss. I told him he shouldn't be kissing me if he was with my friend. This was embarrassing and my naivety showed, having never been kissed before.

Looking at that scenario with a view to changing the outcome, my decision was to have everyone accept the new girl at school.

Next, I remembered myself being raped at twenty-three when I lived overseas. I was forced into something, against my will. The man had a gun and he was in control. Again, my freedom was taken away.

"This is the event that triggered your high blood pressure," the therapist stated.

The incident was very traumatic even though I did have the initiative to memorise the number plate. Looking at changing this event in my mind and body, I visualized myself staying the night with my friends, enabling me to travel home the next day without incident.

I looked at this traumatic event in a kinesiology appointment in 1996, because of recurring dreams 23 years after the incident. This counselling, changed my life appreciably, although at the time blood pressure was not an issue.

My blood pressure rose quite high, after the discovery of Brian's dead body. Having called the police, they treated me as a suspect because there was no-one else in the home. I tend to keep all my faculties together in a crisis and fall apart afterwards. Hours later I was released from all the questioning to go home, with my body feeling frozen in time, which was obviously shock. My appointments were busy the next day and through to the following week, which precipitated the soldier on response, with the added duty to organize a funeral.

On the Thursday morning of the following week, the tears started running down my face like cascades over a smooth rock face. These droplets of tears continued whilst in the shower, covering my cheeks and neck, with the water from the nozzle covering the tears as they rolled over the body. Driving to work there was no release from the wanting torrent of tears, making it quite impossible to work. My whole being held together to perform my important duties, then the grieving process attacked without warning.

Being the executor of his will and with the position of authority to organize the funeral, I performed my duties adequately. It was not until the funeral was over that my blood pressure resumed to normal. The treatment finished.

The changes in the river or the blood system can create dangers to the system, although being aware of our body's fluctuations, can initiate a quick recovery.

My Special Gift

My river of life is on track and running smoothly along its soul's purpose.

I have a special gift of being able to hear spirits talking to me. Sometimes the spirits are standing next to me and other times I am approached while meditating. They appear while I am giving a healing or reading to pass on a message. Spirits are not around me every minute of the day because I clear the energy from each client by protecting myself with white light and healing with purple light.

My mother's communication to me is twofold, one through meditation and also the presence of her energy nearby. I have felt her hand touching mine and her arms around my shoulders to cuddle me. These delicate touches are similar to the feel of a feather.

A couple of months before finishing one of my edits on this book, I was cooking over the gas cooktop when the presence of my mother appeared. Turning around, my mother's energy was to the right of me, then turning to the left of the room, I acknowledged the presence of my father. Immediately the word that came to me was "calamity". I asked my mother what it referred to, nevertheless she wouldn't say. A few weeks later I realised it was in reference to the loss of a family loved one. My parents stayed with me throughout this traumatic period on a daily basis.

One night when teaching a meditation class I experienced my parents lifting me out of the chair and into my lounge where my computer was set up. They both verbalised the need to write every day including weekends, to enable me to finish this book in September. The book was finished in the first few days of September that year.

I have learned that the spiritual messages received aren't always exactly of my understanding. My interpretation can be a little out of sync. Let's face it, if we were given all the answers we wouldn't have any mystery or challenges to look forward to in life. The majority of messages received are given to me years before they actually happen.

Contradictory to the last sentence the following message needed urgent attention. One evening sitting on my comfy recliner lounge, watching an ABC program, out of the corner of my left eye, a bright light caught my attention.

Turning to investigate, I asked: "Is anyone there?"

Immediately the spirit of my father appeared. "Wow! Dad, it's wonderful to see you."

We chatted for a while and then he said: "Can you visit your brother Josh in Melbourne?"

"Yes, I am flying down at Christmas."

"I mean now!"

"Why?"

No answer.

"Do you need me to give him a healing?"

No answer. Even though he didn't speak, my feelings were that Josh needed a healing.

Josh had just finished a health treatment and my thoughts had been to visit him at the end of the year.

"Okay Dad, I'll book to go down in the next few weeks."

He happily said: "Yes, excellent."

We both expressed our love and goodbyes.

The next day I booked my flight to Melbourne, in three weeks and rang Josh to let him know.

Finally, the day arrived with excitement in my veins; as this was the city I was born in, visiting was always stimulating. Lunch arrangements were made with Josh and his family a few days later. My sister, Maureen, invited me to visit her in Mornington, which is only a few suburbs from Josh and his family.

A beautiful day adorned the Sunday of our luncheon. I was driven by Maureen and met my son at the house. There was so much joviality as we each enjoyed the sumptuous meal with a few wines to add to the frivolity.

Before departing I suggested to Josh, "Is Tuesday afternoon a good day for my return to give you a healing?"

"Yes, I'll see you on Tuesday, Lynne."

Tuesday arrived and my sister was working, which meant the train was my transport for the day. I was blessed with a hot coffee and banana bread at my favourite café in Mornington before heading off to see Josh. The weather was a little cool although I enjoyed the relaxing journey.

Hopping off the train and feeling the rain drops starting, my decision was to catch a taxi to his house, with the rain disappearing as I stepped out of the cab. My brother, who was home alone, greeted me at the door and immediately offered refreshments. During the small talk over lunch I interjected to change the subject onto the healing treatment and explain the process.

"This treatment involves me placing my hands above your body and allowing the negative energy to be released. I will also be channelling information to help with your health."

As soon as lunch was finished and the table cleared, my thoughts were that he could remain in his chair as there was no suitable table.

After clearing the room of any negative energy, I stood behind my brother, tuning into his needs. Immediately I was drawn to his heart area where there was a deep secret.

"Josh, very deep inside you there is a broken heart. It is connected to Mum dying so young (I had always suspected this although he never acknowledged it). You blamed yourself for not being there to save her."

* * *

"You need to release this guilt. Our Mother died because she was worn out and it was her time to go."

Instantaneously our Mother's spirit appeared on his left side and she said: "You need to release the guilt of not being there when I died Josh. It was my time and I am happy here."

Suddenly our Father's spirit appeared on the chair next to my brother. I immediately remembered, "I am the Messenger" and that was the reason for me to be here. I felt so thrilled to be able to execute this recovery process.

Father said, "You are my first born son to live. Rest is very important to aid in your recovery. You will live to see your son grow up."

I instantly wrapped my arms around my brother as we both shed tears. Eventually trying to unwrap myself from him, he hung on tight. We stayed in this embrace for many minutes as we both cried tears of joy. Eventually I was able to release my arms from around his shoulders.

This event was so empowering. Josh was so accepting of what had just transpired and extremely grateful. Time is so important for the healing process and also the acceptance of such a huge event.

"Take it easy over the next few days and remember father's words about rest. The more you rest, the more the recovery will be successful."

At that moment his son opened the front door returning from school. I gathered my belongings and hugged them both before embracing my journey to see Brendan, my second brother, before flying home the next day.

There was a huge smile on my face as I flew back to Brisbane; happy at the success of this trip.

I am very grateful for my gifts and hope that this book has given you, the reader, a vision as to why "I am the Messenger."

THE END

www.ingramcontent.com/pod-product-compliance
Lightning Source LLC
Chambersburg PA
CBHW052006090426
42741CB00008B/1580